DID I WIN? BEYOND THE VERDICT

Unleash Your Inner Power with RGD Blueprint

DEDICATION

To my mother, **Barbara Herring,**

You were the foundation of my strength and the source of everything I learned about morality and principles. Even in my darkest times, you pulled me up. You were the one who kept me going, teaching me how to fight, how to stay strong, and how to believe in myself. You are the main reason I realized the power of the **RGD Blueprint—Resilience, Growth Mindset, and Discipline**—and I dedicate this realization to you.

In loving memory of my sister, **Rrapanza Danner**. You were always my best friend and you are deeply missed.

To my late father, **George Herring**. Thank you for always being there, showing me how a man provides for his family and is the steadfast rock they can lean on.

You are all deeply loved and dearly missed. God bless your souls.

TABLE OF CONTENTS

PROLOGUE

THE DAY HELL FROZE OVER

99/98/9999

The world, they say, is a cold, unforgiving place. And hell? According to the preachers, it burns with an inferno that consumes every last shred of hope. But for me, **Alfonse Danner**, these two opposing forces didn't just meet; they collided with a thunderous, soul-shaking **CRACK!** on May 17th, 2022. That was the pivotal day I finally walked out of a Florida prison after twenty-six years and eight months behind concrete walls, cold steel bars, and barbed wire — doing their damnedest to consume every fiber of my being. That was the moment hell officially needed a snow shovel, and by God, I was holding the handle.

"Life," Judge Chet Tharp had decreed back in March 1996, his voice flat, devoid of a single flicker of human emotion, "I will make sure you will no longer prey on society."

I had just turned twenty-six years old, arrested in September 1995, and now, a mere six months later, the gavel fell, sealing a fate I couldn't comprehend. My supposed crime was a non-violent burglary that had somehow been twisted, through legal machinations and arbitrary rules, into a crushing life sentence. This egregious injustice was compounded by a phantom: a gun I never possessed, a weapon allegedly stolen by someone else—a mere specter in a narrative designed to condemn.

They treated me like a monster, a cold-blooded killer, even though not a single person was physically hurt. There was no physical violence. Just a kid from Tampa, caught in the intricate, unforgiving web of a system that seemed less interested in actual justice or rehabilitation, and far more invested in making a brutal, chilling example. Judge Tharp, freshly appointed to the bench, was seemingly eager to make a name for himself, quickly gaining a reputation for outrageously disproportionate sentences. Unknowingly, I became one of his early, tragic examples—trapped by a judge who, years later, would be removed from that very bench for similar ethical and sentencing violations. But for me, **Alfonse Danner,** in that soul-crushing moment, his harsh judgment sealed my fate.

The initial shock of that "Life" sentence was a visceral, physical blow, like a punch in the gut that left me gasping for air in that crowded, echoing courtroom. My brain couldn't compute the words; couldn't reconcile them with the life I believed I had. Then, a raw, all-consuming rage hit me. Hard. I was stunned, my mouth dropped open, unable to think how my life had come to this agonizing precipice. Somehow, I managed to lift my jaw from the floor of that courtroom and unleash. I cursed him—the judge, the silent courtroom, the entire damn system—letting loose a torrent of invective, a volcanic eruption of defiance that would make the most hardened sailor blush.

Judge Tharp, visibly startled by my unbridled outburst, immediately ordered the bailiffs to remove me. They hustled me out, but my fury kept burning. I kept cussing, my voice hoarse, loud enough for every stunned face to hear, down the hallway, through the doors, and into the silence that followed — the silence of a man whose entire future had just been ripped away.

The county jail, already a temporary hell, now felt like a permanent holding cell for an eternity. But the real, terrifying descent began when I was transported to the notorious State of Florida Department of Corrections. That's where reality truly slapped me in the face, not with a guard's fist, but with a deceptively simple piece of paper that made my blood run ice-cold.

"My story took a disorienting twist the very moment I entered the Florida Department of Corrections. Though the court sentenced me under my true, legal name, **Alfonse Danner**, upon my arrival at state prison, my identity was inexplicably, unilaterally erased. All of a sudden, I was known as Tony Jackson—an alias I'd used once upon a time, but one completely unrelated to my current case or sentencing.

The **DOC**, for reasons unknown and never corrected, simply chose to call me by this other name. I spent **nearly 27 years** in that system as Tony Jackson, living under a moniker that wasn't mine. Every piece of mail, every interaction, every official document was addressed to Tony Jackson. Living under an imposed identity for so long blurred the lines of my own sense of self, and when I finally walked free, it genuinely took me months to adjust back to being **Alfonse Danner**. But to add some serious salt to the wound, about a month into my incarceration, my official release date was stamped clearly: **99/98/9999**."

My brow furrowed in disbelief. "What the hell is this?" I muttered to myself, my finger trembling as I pointed at the impossible string of nines and the alien's name. "How am I supposed to meet this date? "An older, grizzled inmate, a man whose face was etched with more years inside than I had been alive, just looked at me. A grim, knowing smile played on his lips. "Son," he drawled, his voice raspy, "that's your release date. Welcome to the system. That's the day hell freezes over." And honestly, that darkly ironic statement became my morbid curiosity for the next twenty-six years: what would hell freezing over truly look like? Would there be little demon snowmen having snowball fights?

Turns out, it looks a lot like **May 17, 2022**— the day I walked free. After nearly twenty-seven years of concrete and steel trying to consume me, after answering to a name that wasn't mine for literally decades, I walked. Free. It was less a typical release and more like a bloody, bare-knuckle brawl for my very soul against a system that thought it had me trapped forever. But I won that appeal, snagged a resentencing, and then—**BAM!** —Just like that, the gate clanged open.

Hot met cold. The two forces collided with a thunderous **CRACK**! that day. What a show. I definitely didn't mind hell freezing over, because when I stepped back into the society, I already knew one undeniable truth: it's a cold, unforgiving world out here. And I was ready for it.

So, you think you've had a bad day? Try staring down a life sentence, being processed under a ghost name that followed you for almost three decades, and getting a monthly "release date" that read: never. While everyone else counted days, I was staring at a permanently blank calendar. My existence was a bureaucratic error, a ghost in the system, a cautionary tale whispered in the dark corners of the penitentiary. Every single month, that piece of paper was a fresh slap in the face, confirming my future was a permanent blank, and my very identity had been erased like I never existed.

But let me reintroduce myself.

You're about to meet **Alfonse Danner**—the dude who cursed out a judge in open court, battled prison guards like it was a contact sport, and then, against all odds, meticulously learned how to program industrial machines behind bars. You'll witness the gut-wrenching losses of a mother and a sister that should have broken me into a million pieces, leaving me just another statistic swallowed by the concrete walls. And then, you'll see how I walked out after twenty-seven years with literally nothing but the clothes on my back, no ID, no proof of existence, and against all logic, built a whole damn life from scratch in less than three years. If that doesn't put your "bad day" into perspective, I don't know what will.

This isn't some self-help fairy tale spun from fluffy theories. This is the unvarnished, no-punches-pulled truth of how I leveraged three fundamental, non-negotiable principles not just to survive hell, but to truly thrive on the other side: **Resilience, Growth Mindset, and Discipline – or RGD.** Think of it as your personal operating system upgrade because most people out there are running on a glitchy, error-prone version, programmed by fear, doubt, and a mountain of self-defeating excuses.

My journey proves that **RGD** is the raw, uncut code for an unbreakable mind. This isn't just my story; it's your blueprint, etched in the concrete dust and hard-won lessons of my life, designed to help you install **RGD** and reprogram your own damn brain for an unbreakable existence.

You're going to hear about the chaos that defined my early days—the mean streets of Tampa, the brief, chaotic stint in the military, a terrifying near-death experience on a jet fighter deck that almost turned me into a permanent resident of the South China Sea. You'll see the self-destructive spiral that followed, landing me in the belly of the beast, caught in Judge Chet Tharp's web. How that same judge-the one eager to make a name off harsh sentences—would later get removed from the bench for the same kind of injustice he dumped on me.

I was a hothead then, full of fire and rage, but I didn't deserve that injustice. I didn't deserve to be treated like a killer when no one got hurt. Even with my flaws, the sentence was disproportionate, inhumane.

The anger was immediate, a burning inferno that consumed me for years. For the first ten years behind bars—especially the first five—that anger festered like an open wound, threatening to poison everything. My mind was a battlefield, chaotic and consumed by bitterness and the overwhelming desire for revenge against the system, against Tharp, against everyone who had played a part. I spent years plotting, resenting, feeling that visceral rage every time I thought of him, or the cold, or the indifferent system that had stolen my life and my very identity. It was a suffocating internal battle, a constant fight against the emotional shackles of resentment that threatened to define my entire existence.

But then something shifted. I got tired of being angry. Tired of wasting energy on people who weren't even thinking about me. Tired of staying stuck while the world kept spinning.

You'll witness the agonizing, often hilarious, journey of self-reflection, a brutal, honest confrontation where I finally had to look in the mirror and admit that I was my own most significant problem. You'll learn how I traded that simmering, destructive rage for razor-sharp focus, how I used every setback—from the terrifying chaos of prison riots to soul-crushing appeal denials, and that monthly, dehumanizing slap-in-the-face **"release date"** under the wrong name—as raw fuel for a relentless, impossible climb. It took about ten long years for the anger to finally subside, for me to fully commit to bettering myself, and to understand that if I didn't truly change, I'd only end up right back where I started, or worse. That's when I stopped just reading books and began living them, realizing the three foundational forces for any proper comeback: **Resilience, Growth Mindset, and Discipline.**

Want to know how I escaped the mental prison long before I walked out of the physical one? Stick with me. I'm going to show you. This book isn't just my story; it's a raw, unfiltered lesson in what happens when you stop making excuses and start taking absolute control of your mind. We all face adversity, a constant, unavoidable force in life. It's the universe's way of hitting you with a shovel, not to bury you, but to see if you'll dig or lie there. This book will show you how to embrace that shovel, how to transform pain into power, and how to forge a mentality of steel that nothing can shatter.

Here's the deal with RGD:

- **Resilience:**

You'll learn the practical wisdom of **Resilience**—Not just about bouncing back. It's about bouncing forward—stronger, smarter, more intelligent, more determined, from every single hit. Life will hit you. That's a guarantee. But **Resilience** is what lets you get up with **purpose**. Think of it as your psychological Armor, allowing you to absorb blows and keep fighting.

Every time I was denied an appeal, every time I was disrespected, overlooked, and forgotten, **Resilience was** what kept me from breaking. I'm not saying you won't feel pain. I'm saying you won't let pain be the end of your story.

Psychologists like Martin Seligman, the father of Positive Psychology, have championed this exact thing. The ability to thrive in the face of adversity. To take your trauma and use it. I didn't just survive prison—I turned it into my proving ground. This isn't about being bulletproof; it's about being bounce-proof.

- **Growth Mindset**

You'll understand the liberating power of a **Growth Mindset**—the unshakeable belief that your capabilities are limitless, that challenges are not roadblocks but profound opportunities for learning and growth. This isn't some wishy-washy positive thinking; it's the scientifically proven perspective championed by **Dr. Carol Dweck** from Stanford, showing that believing you can grow literally rewires your brain for success and perpetual improvement. It means seeing every screw-up as a valuable lesson, not a damning limitation.

Every setback became a lesson. Every failure is a push forward. I went from rage to responsibility, from reaction to reflection.

That mindset? It's how I started teaching myself machine programming in a place that was built to crush dreams.

- **Discipline**

And you'll grasp the foundational necessity of **Discipline**— the consistent, often thankless daily grind that turns impossible dreams into undeniable reality. This focused, unwavering action melds you into the person you need to be. This is the persistent effort that transforms potential into performance, often overlooked but vital for 'self-regulation' and achieving any significant goal. It's about showing up for yourself, even when no one else is watching, especially when no one else is watching.

Together, these three forces—**Resilience, Growth Mindset, and Discipline**—became my foundation.

They turned my rage into **focus**, my pain into **power**, and my sentence into a **second chance**.

My journey proves that no matter where you start, no matter the mistakes you've made, no matter the walls in front of you—or the ones you unwittingly built yourself—you possess the inherent, untapped power to transform your life profoundly.

You'll learn how to transform negative thoughts into unstoppable fuel, how to set realistic goals that accumulate into monumental, undeniable victories, and how to build a circle of influence that consistently elevates you consciously. This isn't theoretical; it's battle-tested in the most unforgiving classroom imaginable.

So, here's the question I want you to ask yourself, right now:

- What's the most enormous wall standing between you and the life you truly want? Is it external, or is it the invisible one you've painstakingly built inside your own head?
- What if the very adversity you're running from, the very pain you're avoiding, is the raw material for your greatest strength and most profound transformation?
- Are you truly ready to stop letting life happen to you and instead start actively making it happen for you?

If you're tired of just surviving and genuinely ready to thrive, to unleash the unbreakable version of yourself, then turn the page. Your upgrade begins now.

CHAPTER 1

I AM LIVING PROOF

The word "life" cracked through the courtroom like a physical blow. Its echo rang in my ears as my world blurred into nausea and disbelief. Not the vibrant, chaotic life I'd known—a reckless mix of street violence and raw adrenaline—but a cold, sterile eternity behind unforgiving bars. I'd danced with death countless times in the streets, a wild ballet of blood and bravado, always believing I was untouchable. I never imagined it would end like this: the cold, dead eyes of Judge Chet Tharp, devoid of any discernible emotion, sealing my fate with the flick of a pen.

Even now, decades later, it makes little sense how **Alfonse Danner**, a kid born into a world of order and love, ended up staring down a sentence meant for true monsters. My childhood was a sanctuary of middle-class stability right there in Tampa, Florida.

My mother, Barbara Herring, was a woman of unwavering faith, profound wisdom, and relentless grace. She instilled in me the non-negotiable power of education and the bedrock importance of morality.

My father, George Herring, a man of quiet strength and principled conviction, taught me the invaluable lessons of hard work and unwavering integrity. We were a close-knit family—my sister, Rrapanza Danner (yes, that's two R's, not a typo), my brother, Samuel Danner, and I—bound in a kind of love I thought would always keep me grounded.

Church pews were as familiar as my bed; I absorbed scripture with the same effortless ease I devoured textbooks, acing tests without so much as a second glance. My family, my teachers, even my friends, all wondered how someone so book-smart could be so bored with school. The simple truth was, knowledge came effortlessly. When I was young, I was a self-professed "geeky nerd"—obsessed with reading, devouring everything from history books to science encyclopedias, often equipped with a telescope or a chemistry kit. By the time I actually arrived at school, much of it felt like mere review. I took that natural intelligence for granted; looking back, I wish I hadn't taken that for granted. It was my first profound mistake.

My mom, — God bless her relentless heart — had one burning dream for me after high school: college. And honestly, I could've aced it. Books were always my strong suit, a world I could effortlessly navigate. But classrooms felt like a suffocating cage, and the very concept of sitting still was a foreign, almost painful, imposition. Traditional school felt like a slow death. But not the school of hard knocks, which I quickly and enthusiastically enrolled in, majoring in "Street Life."

The Unexpected Arrival

Back then, right after high school, I was already running the streets, deep in the hustle and bustle. I was making my own money, flashing it around, feeling like Mr. Big Shot, a young king of my own concrete jungle. My days were a wild blur of buying fresh clothes, adorning myself with flashy jewelry, cruising in new cars, endless partying, and chasing different girlfriends. It was all a dizzying whirlwind of getting drunk, escaping any genuine responsibility, and living for the moment. I was 18, maybe 19 — young, reckless, and full of fire. You know how the rest goes. I always thought I was being smart about it, at least in one crucial area: using condoms to avoid diseases. That was my main, often my only, reason for caution.

My friends and I, we were so wild, so reckless we used to joke, 'Put a hole in a tree, and we'd be ready.' Even if someone felt **"risky,"** we'd sometimes throw caution to the wind, thinking we wouldn't get "burned."

Then, out of nowhere, a word started circulating through my circle, a rumor that felt like a phantom punch to the gut: "I guess I got somebody pregnant." My first, instinctive reaction was a desperate, internal scream: "No, that can't be!" When my daughter's mother first told me directly, her words were tough to swallow, even harder to honestly believe. "No way," I argued, my voice tight with denial. "We only had sex one time!"

As clueless as I was, caught in my self-absorbed world, I couldn't wrap my head around how one single time could possibly lead to an entirely new life. But she was so sure, so certain, and then the devastating realization hit me: I was her first. She hadn't been with anyone else. The denial crumbled, leaving me stunned, disoriented, and utterly scared. I had never, not once, in all my reckless escapades, considered the possibility of getting someone pregnant, even with all the unprotected sex I was having. It never even flickered across my mind—not once.

Despite my overwhelming fear and profound lack of planning, one unshakeable principle my mother had always taught me stuck: I wasn't allowed to walk away. So, from the moment I found out I was going to be a father, I showed up. Before my daughter was even born, I was taking care of things, making sure her mother had whatever she needed, trying to prove, even to myself, that I could be responsible.

When my beautiful baby girl arrived, she was a tiny miracle, the first grandchild on both sides of the family, radiating an innocence that cracked open my hardened shell. We were both so incredibly young, but I did whatever I could, finding every possible way to provide. She was always on my mind, a constant, flickering light, my number one responsibility, my reason to try. I loved her to death and promised myself, with every beat of my heart, to always, always be there for her.

The unexpected birth of my daughter became a moment to press the reset button on my chaotic life. The military, I felt, was the best, perhaps the only, solution. I did what I usually do: tested pretty high on the entrance exams, a familiar flash of that latent intelligence. Next thing I knew, I was a fresh recruit, officially enrolled in the U.S. Navy. My first orders were to boot camp in Orlando, Florida, for initial training (back when they still had boot camp there), and then, very far out, to the sunny, intimidating expanse of San Diego, California.

Could you imagine being sent thousands of miles away to the opposite coast—utterly alone?   I had no family over there; I didn't know a soul, except for a childhood friend and her family, who had moved to Los Angeles. It was weird, being out on my own, adrift, thousands of miles away, constantly missing my family and the familiar streets of Tampa. I had to learn to adapt, to make new friends, to navigate a world utterly alien to me.

This was 1989-1990, and California had a serious, palpable gang problem, a different kind of street code than I was used to. When I left Florida, I was already running from the streets myself, trying to escape the dangerous gravitational pull of that life. But paradoxically, I had no fear; the gangs didn't bother me. They didn't scare or intimidate me. I guess I was ignorant then, didn't fully comprehend the depth of the danger, because I'd lived among it for so long, I'd become so intimately familiar with its rhythms in the streets of my youth. It was wild, a young man from the East Coast dropped into a completely different environment across the country, without the comforting shield of family.

Being in the Navy, specifically assigned to the Air Department, working directly on the flight deck, was a hell of an experience—unlike anything I'd ever known. I was stationed on the USS Ranger, a massive and awe-inspiring aircraft carrier —a floating city of steel and thunder. Its flight deck was an intimidating beast, especially to a newcomer: a sprawling, chaotic landscape of roaring engines and hulking metal, everything compact, planes folded in, precisely parked, a maze of powerful machinery waiting to unleash fury.

At first, I wasn't so sure about it, overwhelmed by the sheer scale and danger, but once I got into the rhythm, once the fear transmuted into respect, it was wild, exhilarating, and truly unforgettable. I saw the world, man—the vibrant chaos of Hong Kong, the raw beauty of the Philippines (twice, including the gritty Subic Bay and Olongapo), the exotic allure of Pattaya Beach in Thailand, the gleaming modernity of Singapore, and the ancient mysteries of Abu Dhabi. My ship took me to places many people only dream of seeing.

I traveled more in those few years than most people do in an entire lifetime, soaking up different traditions and cultures like a sponge. It was absolutely amazing, and I was just a young, excited kid, absorbing it all. That's one thing I truly loved about the military: the chance to visit places many may never see.

Then came the ultimate plot twist: I found myself thrust into the thick of the 1991 Gulf War. I- the kid who hated sitting still in class, was now launching F-14 Tomcats, F-18 Hornets, EA-6B Prowlers, A-6 Intruders, S-3 Vikings (we called them 'Shit Cans'), E-2 Hawkeyes, and C-2 Greyhounds off a flight deck. I was part of the Catapult Crew, strapping multi-million-dollar war machines to the launch rail, sending them screaming into the sky.

Our ship, the USS Ranger, CV-61, was one of the first to open fire, launching those planes that dropped bombs and delivered a whole lot of destruction. It was incredibly dangerous work, high-risk, to the point that we received extra hazard pay, but it was also undeniably exhilarating. We were sending jets into a war zone, directly contributing to the thunder of battle. I was actually in the Persian Gulf itself in 1991, in the heart of the conflict, and yes, I even have a war medal. Yeah, me. It's almost too wild to believe, a jarring contrast to the life I later led, but there it is.

During flight operations, the deck transformed from a static maze into a living, breathing, dangerous organism. When they announced flight ops, the casual crowd thinned, but the organized chaos intensified. It was a terrifying ballet; every crew member knew their precise job, every movement meticulously choreographed, guided by painted safety lines and strict protocols designed to keep them alive. Then came the F-14s, F-18s, EA-6Bs, A-6s, S-3s, E-2s, and C-2s—all the planes coming to life, engines roaring to a deafening crescendo, heat rippling the very air around them like a visible force field. It was incredibly intense and unforgivably dangerous. You had to be on your P's and Q's, acutely aware of every single detail, because one tiny slip, one moment of inattention, could—and often did—cost you your life. When I first started, it was incredibly intimidating —a sensory overload that threatened to overwhelm me.

However, as I learned more and the chaos became familiar, it transformed into an exhilarating dance. I came to truly enjoy it. But the flight deck at night, after flight ops? That's a whole different kind of hell. It's a dark, screaming ballet of jet engines and hulking metal, where the darkness amplifies the roar and the danger. You learn really quick to know where your feet are at all times, to be acutely aware of every inch of space, or you end up just another statistic, crushed beneath a tire or blown into the abyss.

We were hustling to shut down the catapults, jamming these big, heavy rubber slot seals into the hot, steaming trenches that ran the length of the deck. Steam so hot it'd peel paint off metal, and if a plane dripped even a single drop of fuel into that fiery abyss, you got a spontaneous, explosive inferno. So, you moved fast, with desperate urgency, like your very life depended on it, because plane handlers were already swinging jets over those same catapults the moment we were done. Timing was everything; one misstep, or one second too slow, and you became a pancake.

One particular night, I'm deep in it, my back to the rest of the world, flashlight in hand, completely focused on the task. The profound darkness and the heavy flight gear made it tough to see anything beyond my own damn boots. Suddenly, like a collective gasp, everyone around me froze. Guys were hitting the deck, instinctively grabbing onto those heavy metal pad eyes drilled into the carrier floor—the same ones they chained the planes to. My instincts screamed, and I spun around, but it was too late. An F-18, a beast of an aircraft, was turning, its invisible exhaust a roaring, scalding furnace, swinging straight for me. I dove, aiming desperately for a pad eye, anything to anchor myself to the deck, anything to avoid being swept away, but I missed.

The jet wash, a hurricane of hot, unforgiving air, caught me mid-air. I was just a rag doll, weightless and helpless, blown clear across the damn catapult, flying like some kind of pathetic, airborne projectile, until I slammed with bone-jarring force into the catwalk railing. For a terrifying, eternal second, I thought I was going overboard, plummeting into that black, freezing ocean, a thousand miles from anything recognizable, a thousand miles from home. The crew found me, twisted up in the railing, battered but incredibly lucky that steel cage was there. If it weren't for that catwalk, I'd have been a ghost in the South China Sea, another nameless casualty swallowed by the vast, indifferent ocean. I spent some quality time in medical, patched up but profoundly shaken to my core, a new kind of fear etched into my soul.

The Descent Begins: A Different Kind of Battle

After that war, after the relentless intensity of being on that flight deck, after dealing with whatever unspoken trauma the military inevitably burns into me, things started to unravel. I don't know if it was the war itself or just me, but everything started going downhill —a slow, insidious slide into chaos. I eventually received an "other than honorable" discharge, which wasn't a bad conduct discharge or anything particularly severe—just a positive urine test, a minor infraction that still carried consequences. When I returned home from the military, I had no plan, no direction, and no sense of purpose beyond escaping. I thought I'd get some rest and figure things out, but I never gave myself a real chance; I never created a pathway forward. And with no real direction, no guiding star, I gravitated back to what I knew, what felt familiar, what offered a twisted sense of comfort: the streets.

It certainly didn't help-my mind was a mess my head was all screwed up from just leaving the military, carrying unspoken burdens and unprocessed experiences. That's where the heavy drinking truly kicked in, a desperate attempt to numb the confusion and the emptiness.

In the Navy, being away from home, the constant partying and drinking was a whole culture, a twisted way for some guys to cope with the stress and isolation. For me, it became a full-blown, terrifying problem. I was drinking like a fish, teetering dangerously on the edge of becoming a full-blown alcoholic. It was an experience I'll never forget, but one that undeniably marked the beginning of my true, accelerated descent into self-destruction. It was a tragic pattern I saw in far too many guys who came back from that war.

My mom, God bless her heart, used to worry about me when I was out on the streets. She'd hear about the wild, crazy things I did, the dangerous, senseless situations I'd put myself in, and her heart would ache. She just wanted me out of that life, even if, in her quiet desperation, it meant incarceration. She never prayed for a life sentence, of course, that was unthinkable, but she prayed relentlessly for me to get off those treacherous streets, to be safe. She knew, with an almost prophetic certainty, that I needed time away from that destructive environment. I used to be so upset with her for thinking that way, for wanting that for me, seeing it as a betrayal.

Years later, after gaining a better understanding, after walking through my own hell and learning my brutal lessons, I realized with gut-wrenching clarity: she was absolutely right. Where would it have stopped? Probably the graveyard, or a cold slab in the morgue. It's a sad, undeniable truth that it took prison to finally slow me down, to force me to learn, to make me confront myself. But sometimes, whatever it takes is what it takes. I had to accept that for me to truly slow down, learn about myself, advance, and ultimately discover the transformative power of **RGD**.

The street was a brutal, unforgiving teacher that somehow offered a twisted sense of belonging and a false camaraderie. It was a world of extremes, where violence was the universal language, and respect, a fragile commodity, was earned in blood and intimidation. I was drawn to its chaotic energy, its raw and undeniable intensity, in a way that I still struggle to fully comprehend. It was as if I were living two distinct lives: the dutiful son who returned home, and the reckless street warrior who prowled the night.

The adrenaline rush of a fight, the fierce loyalty forged in the crucible of shared danger, the intoxicating illusion of power—they became my addiction, a powerful drug coursing through my veins. I reveled in it, a young fool blinded by the false promise of the streets, convinced I was invincible. It was a world where I felt... alive, in a way that books and classrooms, or the structured boredom of the military, could never offer. A dark, twisted, dangerous kind of alive.

Each fight, each confrontation, each reckless gamble chipped away at the solid foundation of my upbringing, slowly eroding the principles my parents had painstakingly built within me. Fistfights escalated into brutal bar brawls, and bar brawls spiraled into something far more sinister, far more deadly. Guns, once distant objects, became an extension of my hand, and shootouts, terrifying dances with death, became an unnerving norm. I was losing myself, piece by piece, a slow, agonizing disintegration of identity. The line between right and wrong blurred, then vanished altogether, consumed by the shadows. I was utterly consumed by a world of violence, where survival was the only virtue, and every single day was a battle for dominance, a fight to prove my worth. I was becoming the very monster my parents had warned me against, the same force that Judge Tharp would later condemn

The Life Sentence: The Courtroom Outburst and a Stolen Identity

The judge's words slammed into me like a physical blow. "Life..." The sound echoed in the cavernous courtroom, stripping away any lingering illusion of escape, any thread of hope. His face, etched with a cold, absolute finality, is burned into my memory, a permanent scar. I remember the courtroom, the air thick with a silence so profound it roared in my ears, louder than any jet engine. My vision blurred, tears stinging. I scanned the crowd, a sea of blurred, indifferent faces, until my eyes locked on my mother. Her face... that's the image that haunts me still, a mixture of profound shock, agonizing grief, and a raw, silent pain no parent should ever have to endure. I couldn't bear to see her suffer, couldn't bear for her to witness my final desperate act. In a twisted act of... something—I don't know if it was defiant rage or a broken heart—I screamed at her to close her ears. I couldn't let her hear what came next.

The words erupted from me, a torrent of raw rage and unbridled despair, spitting venom at the judge, the system, the cold, indifferent world that brought me here. They were ugly, profane, a searing reflection of the ugliness that had consumed me, the fire that raged within. I wanted to lash out, to inflict some fraction of the pain I felt, to make them understand the depth of my desolation. The bailiffs swarmed, their hands rough as they dragged me away, but I felt nothing, absolutely nothing. Just a hollow, echoing emptiness where my future used to be. Behind those sterile walls, stripped of everything, I was left with nothing but the wreckage of my life. Anger, bitterness, regret—they were my constant companions, the suffocating weights around my neck.

I blamed everyone but myself, a furious prisoner of my own making, trapped not just by concrete and steel, but by the far heavier chains of my own destructive choices. I was in hell, and I didn't have the first clue how to get out.

My supposed "new life" behind bars kicked off exactly how you'd expect: with a full tank of white-hot, consuming rage. If I were a hothead outside, prison just cranked the dial to eleven, turning me into a walking inferno. The bitter irony of getting a life sentence for a non-violent crime, for a stolen gun that was never used, just kept twisting the knife deeper into my soul. And to add insult to injury, I wasn't even the one who swiped the damn thing. That injustice festered, making me even more bitter, a walking, talking powder keg of resentment and fury, waiting for the slightest spark.

But here's the kicker, the kind of bureaucratic absurdity that makes you want to punch a wall: they didn't even sentence me under my real name. No, they stuck me with "Tony Jackson," an alias I'd used once, probably on a whim, in some forgotten street shuffle, a casual deception in a world full of them. The court knew my real name, hell, everyone knew my real name, but the Department of Corrections? They filed, documented, and branded me as "Tony Jackson." For twenty-six years and eight months, I spent my entire time inside living under a ghost name, a legal phantom, an erased identity. It was a constant, insidious, psychological slap in the face. It didn't make sense. They knew it wasn't Alfonse Danner, but they flat-out refused to fix it, trapping me in a bureaucratic nightmare.

And to add more insult to injury, every single month, they'd hand out a gain time sheet. For every other inmate, it was a precious countdown, a tangible reminder of their impending release date. Perhaps it read "01/20/2021" or something more concrete, a beacon of hope. Mine? Reads 99/98/9999. An imaginary release date, a date that could never be reached, a monthly paper slap reminding me I was here forever, a permanent resident of their personal hell. It was a devastating, soul-crushing blow every single time.

After a while, I just stopped looking, tearing the damn things up and tossing them in the trash, refusing to acknowledge the cruel joke. This constant, crushing reminder, layered on top of being "Tony Jackson," piled more fuel onto the bonfire of my anger, making me even more convinced the system was rotten to its core, designed to dehumanize and destroy.

So, if I cursed out a judge in open court, what the hell did a couple of prison guards think they were gonna do to me? Send me to time out? Couldn't get much worse than "life," right? Following the rules? Please. I didn't give a damn about going to "**the hole**"—that solitary confinement cell. They put me on disciplinary treatments, locked me up by myself, whatever.

My official status was "disrespectful," and frankly, I earned it with every fiber of my being. If a guard gave me attitude, I gave it right back, usually with interest, adding a few choice words of my own. Hell, sometimes I just beat them to the punch and unleashed a verbal barrage before they even opened their mouths. Confinement became my second home, a strange, quiet sanctuary from the general population's noise —a place where I could actually find a moment of peace, a moment to stew in my own rage. The word quickly spread: "That guy? Yeah, he's the new hothead." And I wore that reputation like a badge of honor, a defiant shield against a system that sought to break me.

In fact, the news of my courtroom outburst spread faster than prison gossip, traveling through the grapevine like wildfire. Down the hall in the confinement cell, a guy with a smuggled newspaper yelled down the wing, his voice echoing in the confined space, "Hey, Pop! You made the newspaper! You cussed that judge out, man! Tell everybody in the streets you're a hero!" Yeah, a hero for going out in a blaze of glory, for a moment of raw, uncaged defiance. That's the kind of twisted fame prison offered: a fleeting, bitter recognition in a world that had forgotten my real name.

In that place, I was all heart and fire—a restless spirit that refused to die. A lot of people looked at me as someone who was ready to stand up and fight at the drop of a dime, someone who wouldn't back down. I wasn't the type to start trouble; I didn't begin sh**, but I made damn sure I ended it. If someone wanted to start something with me, I was going to do my best to make sure it ended right there, wholly and decisively. Most people stayed out of my way, sensing the volatile energy I carried, and I earned a certain, unspoken respect during my time in prison, probably because of the sheer, raw way I walked in there. For those first five years, I was a maniac, truly wild, and didn't give a f**

Mom's Persistent Light and the Turning Point

But even in that swirling vortex of anger, that suffocating cloud of rage, there was one constant, one unyielding beacon of light: my mom, Barbara Herring. She never stopped showing up. That wise, persistent woman still radiated faith and hope for the son everyone else had written off — even me. It was soul-crushing, seeing her face, knowing the depth of the pain I'd put her through, the worry I'd etched onto her features. But she never gave up. She'd sit across from me, her eyes filled with a love that transcended the steel mesh, always pushing, always telling me to "hold my stock," to stop blaming the world for my situation and, instead, start owning my choices. "Pop," she'd say, using my childhood nickname, her voice gentle but firm, "the reason you're in this position? It's on you. And no matter what, you gotta start looking at yourself in the mirror and standing up to yourself."

Other prisoners, the older, wiser heads who'd seen it all, tried to talk sense into me, too. "You're smart, man," they'd say, shaking their heads, "but you can be dumber than a bag of rocks." That's what they told me, a brutal, honest assessment. It didn't make sense at first. Smart? Yeah. Dumber? Nah, I was smart. But it took a while, a long, humbling while, for their words to actually sink in, for that truth to penetrate the thick wall of my arrogance. They were right. As the years stacked up, one grim, monotonous year after another, the message became impossible to ignore, echoing my mother's unwavering plea: I needed to get my act together.

I remember the day hope walked a tightrope, teetering precariously over the abyss of my despair. It was about my first denial from the Appellate Court. I'd invested not just a few thousand dollars in a lawyer, an exorbitant sum for a prisoner, but every ounce of desperate faith I had left, every shred of belief in a future outside these walls. I believed this was it. This lawyer. This appeal. My undeniable ticket home. I was going to win. My case would be overturned, and I'd be back out there, back with my precious daughter, back to life, to freedom, to simply being again.

In prison, legal mail wasn't like anything else. Regular mail just hit your dorm, no fanfare, just tossed into a pile. But legal mail? That came from a special building, a designated, highly secure room, served at a specific, almost sacred time, usually around 1 PM. It was a ritual, a formal handoff meant to ensure you couldn't claim you never got it, a document so important it demanded respect. Every single time my name was called for legal mail, a knot would twist in my gut, a familiar clenching of fear. But this time, it was different. This time, it felt like my entire future, my very existence, hung precariously in that single, sealed envelope.

I remember the legal mail call-out. My name echoed through the compound, a sudden, jarring sound. I was on a big compound, and the legal mailroom was at the front, in the administration building, a long, exposed walk across the yard. That walk felt like an eternity, every step heavy, laden with anticipation and a chilling, underlying fear that threatened to overwhelm me. My heart was a frantic drum in my chest, pounding a wild rhythm against my ribs, so loud I thought everyone could hear it. I tried desperately to calm myself, to breathe, to find some semblance of peace, but the warring forces of hope and dread waged an agonizing battle inside me.

The line stretched out before me, an interminable procession of anxious men. Each man ahead of me, receiving their own fate, seemed to move in excruciatingly slow motion, every gesture amplified by my desperate impatience. I wanted to scream. To push. To tear through the line and grab my envelope. Anything to end the wait.   But I knew better. That would land me in the box, in solitary confinement, and this, more than any other moment, was absolutely not the time to lose my cool, not when the answer I desperately needed was so tantalizingly close. So, I waited, a stoic mask hiding the turmoil within. My turn finally came. I signed the paper, the standard receipt acknowledging I'd received my legal mail, my hand trembling slightly, betraying the calm I feigned.

I clutched the envelope, thick with dense, indecipherable legal jargon I barely understood, and turned away from the line. I wanted nothing more than to find somewhere quiet, to sit down, to absorb the news in privacy, to brace myself. But I couldn't. I literally could not hold it for another second. My hands moved before I could stop them, clawing at the rigid seal.   I ripped open the envelope, my eyes scanning frantically, desperate for the word, the phrase, the sign that I was free, that this nightmare was over. I envisioned my daughter's face, felt the warm sun on my skin, and heard the distant laughter of my friends, anticipating my release and my glorious return to life, to having a good time again.

And then I saw it. Amidst the legal mess I barely understood, my eyes found the verdict. In big, stark letters, undeniable, crushing, a single word that shattered my world: **DENIED**.

My world crumbled. **Denied.** The word hit like a blow to the chest, knocking the air out of me. I sat there, stunned, drowning in a vacuum of despair. I didn't know what to do. Should I flip out? Hit something? Cause a scene to land in confinement—just to be alone and try to calm the hell down? The anger was a wildfire, instantly consuming everything, the anxiety a suffocating blanket that pressed down on my chest. It cut so deep, so profoundly, into the very core of my being. All the emotions churned – disbelief, furious rage, and a gut-wrenching despair that threatened to swallow me whole.

And that wasn't the last time. A few months later, it happened again. And again, then again. After the fourth or fifth denial, each one a fresh stab to my soul, I was utterly disgusted. So beaten down, so emotionally battered, I didn't know what to do, what to say, what to feel anymore. That's when something inside me finally broke, irrevocably, utterly shattered. But in the wreckage of that breakdown, something unexpected began to rise—**Resilience**. I remember dropping to my knees. The concrete floor felt cold and hard against my skin, a stark reminder of my harsh reality. I started to pray, a desperate, guttural plea. "Please, God," I whispered, tears finally flowing, a torrent of release, "Please, do not let me die in here. Please, do not let me die in here. I will do everything to better myself, to do the right thing, to honor you. Just please, don't let me die here, God."

That feeling alone, the raw, terrifying reality that I could be stuck in here for the rest of my life, that it could be so easy for me never to get out, to vanish into this system... when that chilling realization finally sunk in, that's when I truly started taking things seriously. That's when I truly began to understand what my mom had been telling me all those years, what an angel she truly was, seeing a path I refused to acknowledge. This was the turning point. This was the moment the comeback began.

From Rage to Resilience: The Grind

That's when the real change began, not in some dramatic explosion, but in a silent, soul-weary decision that barely made a sound, even to me. I started looking for classes, anything that could pull me away from the constant chaos and the heavy, suffocating despair. I threw myself into anger management and self-improvement courses with a fire I didn't fully understand—part desperation, part hunger to survive. And then, the books. Actual books about bettering yourself, about human psychology, about overcoming adversity.

Believe it or not, I would walk into the prison library and tear through books on psychology, self-help, and Resilience like a starving man. I liked to study human behavior, the intricate mental processes of thinking and understanding the 'why' behind actions. These books opened up something profound in me, a new chamber of understanding, an insight into why I had done what I did, and more importantly, how I could actually fix it, how I could reprogram myself. I began applying what I learned—how I spoke, how I responded, how I carried myself—and slowly, things started shifting. My thoughts got sharper. My days felt less like battles and more like chances.

My church background, that early foundation my mother had built, suddenly resurfaced, guiding me with its familiar rhythms. I started praying, really praying, earnestly asking God for guidance, for the strength to be truly stronger, to transform. And it worked. The prison, in its own twisted, brutal way, became my classroom, teaching me a whole lot about myself and the world.

Taking those first steps, making that conscious, agonizing decision to change, was like a key turning in a rusty, long-locked door. Things slowly, incrementally, started to open up. My vision cleared. I began to understand myself, not just the angry, defiant façade I presented to the world, but the complex, vulnerable person underneath. And once I truly understood myself, I could begin to grow. However, growth isn't a one-time event; it's a relentless, ongoing process. It demands unwavering **Discipline**. I had to stay committed, day in and day out, to continually push myself and strive to be better, even when the urge to revert to old habits was overwhelming.

I began studying, acquiring new skills with a ferocious hunger and a relentless pursuit of knowledge. That pursuit even landed me a coveted job in a special prison vocational program. I learned to operate **CNC** machines, writing intricate G-codes that resembled a strange, new industrial poetry, translating designs into tangible reality. I learned **CAD**, computer-aided drafting and design, while working for a furniture company, where I even designed pieces and saw my ideas come to life. I was absorbing manufacturing and design skills I never knew existed, skills I never thought I'd have an interest in.

I learnt that when you truly put your mind to something, when you commit, almost anything is possible. These skills weren't just practical; they fundamentally changed me. They calmed me down, shifting my perspective from chaos to precision, and showing me abilities I didn't even know I possessed —a hidden reservoir of potential. I'd always taken my ability to learn, to retain knowledge, for granted, a casual superpower. Now, slowing down and actually looking at myself, I began to see my self-worth —a deep, quiet appreciation for my capabilities.

The Legal Grind and Unyielding Hope

This new focus, this sharpened mind, also honed my resolve for another battle: my seemingly hopeless legal case. I dove into studying law voraciously—desperate to learn how to fight, how to appeal, and how to untangle the legal maze that had trapped me. It was a brutal, incredibly uphill climb—years of denials piled up, each one a heavy stone on my chest. I poured money into lawyers who gave me nothing but more rejections, more heartbreak. The word **"denied"** echoed like a cruel refrain, again and again, to the point where the first few times nearly broke me, stripping me of every ounce of hope. But eventually, I just went numb. Getting another **"DENIED"** from the appeals court became as unremarkable as the morning count, a routine disappointment rather than a soul-crushing blow.

But that numbness, though, wasn't resignation. It was a weird, almost paradoxical kind of Resilience. I started to understand adversity in a profoundly different way. You don't just give up. You fight through it. You stay resilient. So, I kept filing, kept studying, kept learning more, refusing to yield to the system's relentless pressure. I knew, deep down, with an unwavering conviction, that the deal I got was unfair, a gross miscarriage of justice. That unshakeable conviction drove me to dig deeper, to understand the law, to figure out precisely how to present my case in court and win. It wasn't easy. It wasn't an overnight revelation. It took a hell of a lot of fighting, a lot of grinding, a relentless, solitary battle of wits and willpower. But I never, ever gave up.

The Unexpected Coach and a Different Kind of Fight

Even amidst the grinding routine of self-improvement and the hard lessons learned in steel and concrete, some parts of me just couldn't be caged. I'd always been a natural-born leader, the kind of guy who naturally ends up at the front of the pack, for better or worse, drawing others to me. So, it made sense that I stepped into coaching right there behind bars. Sports—football, softball, basketball—were a big damn deal in my institution, a pressure-cooker arena for guys to blow off steam, release pent-up aggression, and, if they were lucky, forget where they were for an hour or two, truly escaping the grim reality.

When I first started coaching, it was a rough learning curve. The leadership part? Easy. But trying to get a bunch of hardened cons, each with their own wild attitudes and even wilder pasts, to work as one cohesive unit, to put aside individual egos for a common goal? That was a whole different ballgame, a constant negotiation of wills. It took a year of screaming, cajoling, and probably a few near-brawls on the field and court, but eventually, I ironed out the kinks and found the right buttons to push. Results spoke for themselves.

I became one of the best damn coaches on the compound, racking up championships like they were candy, celebrated for my strategic mind. And yeah, I was a hell of a player too, long after I should've stuck to the sidelines, fueled by an old competitive fire. I kept playing until age, and those slow-healing prison injuries finally tapped me out, forcing me to embrace the coaching role truly. Sports became my lifeline, my only authentic outlet in a world designed to grind you down, a place where I could still feel the rush of competition and the satisfaction of victory.

The Call That Shattered Everything

Even with my new focus, my newfound purpose, and the burgeoning strength I was building, life has a funny, cruel way of reminding you who's really in charge. My mom, bless her persistent soul, and my sister were still my constants, visiting whenever they could, their faces a comforting balm. Mom, though, I could see it clearly with each visit. Her health was fading, battling cirrhosis of the liver, a relentless enemy. Each visit, the vibrant light in her eyes seemed a little dimmer, her frame a little frailer, a quiet erosion taking place.

Then came December 2007. I was out on the football field, in the middle of a game, fully absorbed in the moment, when the intercom crackled to life, slicing through the cheers and shouts. "Inmate Jackson, report to the chapel!" Guys on the sideline were shouting, "Hey Pop, they callin' you!" A chilling, undeniable fear snaked down my spine. The chapel? Throughout all my years inside, the chapel never called out to you for good news. My stomach knotted, a cold, heavy dread settling deep within me. Every step across that yard felt heavy, each thought a lead weight in my head. What the hell did they want? Fear, dread, a cocktail of raw, agonizing emotion churned inside me. I was terrified.

I walked into the chapel, the air thick with an ominous silence, and the chaplain didn't mince words; his face was grim. "Got some bad news, son. It's about your mom." That was it. The world tilted, spun on its axis, and shattered. I was about to break down right there, the tears already stinging, but he cut me off. "You need to call your brother. Here's his number." I stumbled to the phone, my fingers fumbling, my vision blurring, as I prayed it wasn't what I thought, praying for a reprieve. Then I heard my brother, Samuel Danner's, voice, cracking with unshed tears, and he confirmed it, the words barely audible: Mom was gone.

A Pain I Didn't Know I Could Feel

I don't think I'd cried since I was eleven or twelve, after one of Mom's legendary whooping, her tough love - a temporary sting. I honestly thought my tear ducts had just packed up and retired, rusted shut from disuse. But that day, they proved me spectacularly, painfully wrong. I balled up, curled into a trembling knot of pain, and cried like a newborn, like a child utterly lost and alone. I didn't even care who saw, didn't care about my reputation, about the watchful eyes of guards or inmates. The pain was physical, a heartbreak so profound it hollowed me out, leaving an echoing void where my anchor had been. It was, without a doubt, the worst feeling of my entire life.

I was broken. Utterly, completely broken, beyond repair, or so it felt. I spent three days stuck on my bunk, a hollowed-out zombie, unable to move, unable to think, barely able to breathe. My job, which had become a source of unexpected pride and purpose, was understood. They told me to take the week off, no questions asked, a rare act of empathy in that unforgiving place. Slowly, agonizingly, I picked myself up, piece by shattered piece. I had to. Not only had I lost the one person who never stopped believing in me, the one person I could always count on, but I couldn't even go to her funeral. Couldn't see her one last time, couldn't say goodbye, couldn't honor her. She was the anchor, the person who got on my case when I was wrong, but never, ever left my side; her love was an unyielding fortress. And now she was just... gone. Then, in 2012, another devastating blow: my father passed away, adding another layer of grief to an already heavy soul.

The Next Blow and Unbreakable Spirit

My sister, Rrapanza Danner, though, stepped up with a fierce resolve. No one could ever truly replace Mom, but my sister became my new rock, my steadfast pillar in a world that

53

constantly threatened to crumble around me. She was family, a constant, loving presence, a fierce protector. She was the brain, the organizer, always calling my other family members and friends, rallying them to visit me, ensuring I felt connected to the outside world, that I wasn't forgotten. She was always worried, constantly checking in, her love a warm blanket against the prison's chill. She visited every other week, bringing other family members, my niece, a constant reminder of the world outside, of the enduring love that still existed for me, a flickering candle in the darkness.

She truly stepped into Mom's role—caring for me with relentless, selfless devotion, always making sure I had what I needed. She was a fierce supporter, refusing to let me sink into despair.

My brother, **Samuel Danner**, was a little different. Don't get me wrong, we were close, incredibly close family. But his burgeoning profession had him incredibly busy; he was on his way to becoming a principal and was intensely focused on that demanding path. Still, every chance he got, he made sure to visit me, or he would always send me books, knowing how much I loved to read and how much I devoured knowledge. He did the best he could, and he did a lot for me, and I love him for it, understanding the pressures he faced.

Then, on the Fourth of July, a day meant for celebration, the universe delivered another gut-punch, a cruel twist of fate. My sister passed away.

That was the worst devastation I'd ever experienced, period. It was devastating enough to lose my sister, but then to lose my best friend, the one who had bravely stepped into Mom's shoes, the one who had so fiercely championed me, my heart was shattered into a million irreparable pieces. Each time, with each unbearable loss, I had to bounce back, had to become stronger, even though the pain was so profound it felt physically intolerable. I missed their funerals, couldn't be there for them, couldn't say my final goodbyes, couldn't mourn properly. My sister died suddenly, unexpectedly, a shock that reverberated through my core. However, I had to keep going; I had no other choice.

As I learned and grew stronger, with the years passing, I began to understand myself even more deeply, to recognize what truly mattered and what I needed to do to keep moving forward. I learned how to avoid problems and steer clear of trouble, not just physically, but mentally. It was a conscious, daily effort, a constant refinement of my new self.

Freedom and a New Identity: The Ultimate Test of Resilience

Through all the adversity, through the shattering losses, through the unending grind of concrete and steel, I leaned on **Resilience**, cultivated a **Growth Mindset**, and embraced **Discipline**. Those three foundational pillars didn't just help me survive; they fundamentally changed my mentality, rewiring my very perception of what was possible. They showed me, unequivocally, that I could accomplish anything I set my mind to, no matter how insurmountable the odds. I now live in a state of mind where I genuinely believe in myself, understand my own worth, and recognize the immense power within me. Even though I was sentenced to life under a ghost name and lost the most important people in my world, the very anchors of my soul, I still prevailed.

Then, on **May 17, 2022—after almost 27 grueling years inside**—hell froze over. I walked out. And the lessons didn't stop there; in fact, the re-entry into the free world presented its own unique set of absurd, almost Kafkaesque, challenges. I didn't have a driver's license, a valid ID, or a Social Security card. All my official paperwork, my entire verifiable identity, was gone. Because I'd been **"Tony Jackson"** for nearly three decades, my prison ID was utterly useless on the outside. There was no official proof that Alfonse Danner, the American citizen, even existed. It was as if I were a ghost in the system, even on the outside, a phantom navigating a world that demanded proof of life. Immigrants from other countries, with their own complex paths, ironically, had a better chance of quickly obtaining some official ID than I did.

It was hard at first, a relentless, frustrating uphill battle against bureaucracy and indifference, but fueled by the **RGD** I had forged, I absolutely refused to give up. I wasn't actually born in America, as you may have noticed, but in Germany. Both of my parents were born in America, which unequivocally makes me an American also. Yes, a Black German-American or a Black American-German. Either way, I am a U.S. citizen by birthright.

My father was in the military, stationed overseas in Germany, and I was born in a German hospital off-base, a place that has since been torn down. This technically made me a German citizen by birth. Still, due to my parents' American citizenship and the circumstances of my birth while my father was on duty, I am unequivocally an American citizen. So, the fact that I, an American citizen, couldn't even prove my American citizenship or get a simple

ID after decades in a system that claimed to know everything about me? That's the real punchline to this whole damn joke, a testament to the absurd challenges I continued to face.

CHAPTER 2

THE BLUEPRINT FOR THE

UNBREAKABLE MIND

The concrete walls around me didn't just hold my body captive; they initially echoed the mental prison I had built long before I ever got locked up... That first raw, brutal period inside—what I now call the "Cage of Rage"—was a stark, unforgiving mirror of the chaotic streets I'd left behind. My defiance, my visceral refusal to bow to authority, my constant, often senseless battles with the guards—it was all a desperate, misguided attempt to prove I was still alive, me, even as the system relentlessly tried to erase me under a ghost name. I was smart, no doubt about it, but as those old heads in prison, with their weary wisdom, bluntly pointed out, I was also "dumber than a bag of hammers" when it came to truly understanding myself, my actions, and their devastating consequences. In my furious blindness, I blamed the system, the judge, society, everyone, and everything but the one man in the mirror who held the actual keys to my liberation.

That courtroom scream—pure rage and pain—didn't help me. It confirmed everything the judge already believed: I was a threat, not worth saving - an unrepentant menace. It was a cruel self-fulfilling prophecy, a public testament to my profound inability to see my own pivotal role in my predicament. My military experiences, particularly the relentless intensity of the Gulf War and the constant vigilance required in other dangerous deployments, had undeniably hardened me, forged a raw resilience. But they had also, paradoxically, closed my eyes to the intricate nuances of civilian life, to the profound importance of emotional accountability, and to the vital distinction between controlled aggression and self-destructive rage.

My relationships with my mother, Barbara Herring, my sister, Rrapanza, and my brother, Samuel, were complex and often strained beneath the surface of our deep familial love. I loved them deeply, fiercely even, but my inability to communicate effectively, my tendency to lash out, to externalize blame, made those connections incredibly difficult to maintain, especially from behind the insurmountable barriers of concrete and steel.

As the years dragged on, each day bleeding into the next, a colder kind of terror crept into my awareness. I saw the faces of the guys who'd been inside for fifteen, twenty years—vacant stares, their eyes like windows to empty rooms, minds lost in the echoes of their own endless confinement. They were institutionalized, stripped of their spirit, hollowed out, often unable to hold a normal conversation or even string a coherent thought together. I looked at them, truly looked, and I saw a chilling, starkly possible future for myself. I refused, with every fiber of my being, to let that happen to me. I was terrified of losing my mind, of becoming another nameless statistic in the silent, insidious war that waged relentlessly inside these walls, a war for the soul. That fear, that absolute horror of mental deterioration, was the undeniable catalyst. It forced me to pause, to listen, truly listen, for the first time, and to finally, agonizingly, look at myself with unblinking honesty.

The Uncomfortable Mirror: Mastering Self-Reflection

Before I could truly embrace growth, before I could even conceive of transformation, I had to master the brutal art of self-reflection. This was a monumental challenge, especially when I'd been walking around with this deep-seated, almost unconscious sense of entitlement—this corrosive belief that the world owed me something, that I was a victim of circumstances beyond my control. Figuring out that profoundly uncomfortable truth, realizing that "the world doesn't owe you anything, the world doesn't owe you shit," was absolutely crucial to even begin chipping away at the foundation of my biased mindset, to even begin being truly self-reflective. It's incredibly hard because it demands stripping yourself bare, being brutally, unforgivingly honest with the most difficult person to confront: yourself.

A lot of people don't truly understand self-reflection because they still cling to a biased mindset, a distorted lens through which they view their own actions. And when you're biased, when you're not being truly honest and truthful to yourself about your flaws, your mistakes, your contributions to your own predicament, it's impossible to see real self-reflection, impossible to truly see yourself.

I used to constantly butt heads with the guards, finding myself in screaming arguments and ending up in confinement all the time. I just didn't like the rules; they felt like arbitrary impositions designed to control me. They were the rules, legitimate and clear, but I'd argue about them anyway, even when they were perfectly reasonable.

I'd deliberately break the rules and then get furious about getting caught, a twisted logic born of defiance. I used to beat the police to the punch, getting mad about breaking the rules myself, as if their reaction was the primary offense. I was just ready for a battle, primed for a fight at any moment, because I had carried that deep-seated baggage, that street-forged animosity towards authority, right into prison with me. From the beginning, I had this sour taste in my mouth, a cynical, confrontational attitude, even when I was dead wrong. It was hard for me to see it, to own it, because I was constantly blaming someone or something else for my predicaments.

No matter what, I still found myself in bad positions, caught in cycles of conflict and punishment, and I just couldn't understand why, couldn't see my own role in it.

And it wasn't just authority figures who triggered me. Even if another inmate said something, anything, about my football team—I was a real die-hard, big-time Tampa Bay Buccaneers fan, and still am—and it was something I didn't like, I was ready to fight. It sounds stupid, right? Petty, childish, because it's just a game. But to me, in that confined, hyper-masculine world, it felt like more than a game; it felt like a direct challenge to my identity, my loyalty, my self-worth. Those were my flimsy reasons, my flimsy justifications, for a lot of little, dumb things that inevitably got me into big trouble. It was incredibly hard for me, in my arrogance and anger, to see that I was fundamentally hot-headed and had some very real, unresolved issues fueling my destructive behavior.

To be truly self-reflective, you have to strip yourself down, layer by painful layer, until you're left with the unvarnished truth. That's arguably the hardest thing to do in life: to actually see yourself as the bad guy when, in a situation, you are the bad guy. A lot of the time, we're not accepting of it, we recoil from that uncomfortable truth. But that's something you have to do. You have to take a long, hard, unflinching look at yourself. You have to stop coming up with excuses, stop thinking about anything else, stop the endless internal justifications. You have to shut everything out—the noise of the world, the whispers of ego—and just stare at yourself, truly stare, and think about all the dumbest things you've done, some of the things you even thought were right at the time.

Look at it raw, objectively, as if someone else were doing these things, saying these words to you. How would you feel? Sometimes, when you put yourself in their shoes, then and only then can you truly see where you're wrong, where you contributed to the problem. Then you can truly see yourself, because now you're looking at it in reverse, like looking into a mirror, but from the other side. That's what self-reflection is. Just put yourself on the other side.

Once you start seeing this, once that raw, uncomfortable truth begins to sink in, you begin to understand yourself a little better, a little more deeply. It takes a while, a long, patient process. First, it may start small, just fleeting glimpses of your own culpability, but then, as you keep practicing, it's almost like learning to meditate. You start off with brief moments, but then you just keep practicing and practicing, making it a daily habit.

After a while, you become better and better with it; it becomes almost natural, an ingrained part of your thinking process. The same thing happens with changing yourself and being more self-reflective. With consistent practice, little by little, you start to see the difference, you'll start seeing how much better you become, how much clearer your vision is, because now you truly see yourself for what you really are—flaws and all. Once you can see yourself like this, with brutal honesty, and you can hold yourself accountable for your actions, that's when you can truly begin to grow your mind, to build your unbreakable self.

My mom's words, the ones that had bounced off the steel walls of my heart for so long, started to penetrate, to finally find purchase. "Pop," she'd said, her voice a steady drumbeat of truth, "the reason you're in this position? It's on you. You gotta start looking yourself in the mirror and standing up to yourself." She was right. All my rage, all my defiance, all my self-pitying tantrums—they weren't changing my sentence. They weren't getting me out of this concrete box. They were just cementing me deeper into the misery, making me an even tighter prisoner of my own mind. I was stuck. The only way out was through. And the only way through was to change the one thing I actually had control over: my own mind.

This arduous journey to accountability started long before prison, though I didn't recognize it then, blinded by my youth and arrogance. For example, I used to skip school—a lot. Like I said, I was pretty good at school; I'd just show up, take the test, and most times I'd ace it, a natural academic without the **discipline** to match. So, a lot of times I'd skip out of school and miss classes because, you know, I wasn't really "there" mentally, my attention drawn elsewhere. When I was young, still in high school, I had a car, a symbol of my premature freedom.

Many times, if my mom, Barbara Herring, found out I skipped school, she'd decide to take my keys. When she took my keys, it really angered and upset me, a perceived infringement on my independence. I'd be mad and would still do something else equally foolish that would piss her off, trapped in a cycle of rebellion. I just didn't understand why she took my keys—those were my car keys, my symbol of freedom. I wasn't looking at the fundamental point that I was skipping school with this car. I was getting in this car and taking off to the streets instead of going to class. So, that was her way of punishment, a logical consequence, stopping me from easily just getting in my car and taking off to the streets. It showed I wasn't responsible enough with that car to prioritize my education.

But to me, at that time, I just didn't see it like that, unable to connect my actions to her consequences. It was hard for me to see it, hard for me to hold myself accountable at all. And she'd always tell me, with exasperated love, "You're in my house, you ain't grown," because I was like 16 or 17 years old, acting like a fully independent adult. It was hard for me to see myself, then, as the source of my own problems, to understand the causal chain of my choices.

One day, after I got my keys back from my momma, fresh from another punishment. I was still pissed off about her taking them, still seething, but I was young and dumb, not seeing her profound wisdom, just thinking she was being mean, controlling my life. I came home and, in a fit of adolescent pique, told my sister, Rrapanza, and my brother, Samuel, that I was packing my clothes and leaving. They looked at me confused, worried, "Pop, what are you doing? Where are you going?" I told them, with a dramatic flourish of my teenage arrogance, "I'm out of here. Tell Mama I'm grown." And I just left, just like that, slamming the door on my stable, loving home.

It was crazy, utterly irrational. I left because I was mad, she was taking my keys, mad she was trying to make me responsible, punishing me for skipping school, for jeopardizing my future. It was outrageous, a childish tantrum, but that's how a young and foolish kid thinks, how irresponsible I was at the time, utterly devoid of foresight. I wasn't thinking about the devastating consequences. I left without a plan, with nothing but the clothes on my back and a head full of stubborn pride. I made myself homeless. I was

17, still in school, and I literally made myself homeless, exchanging the comfort of my bed for the cold, lonely anonymity of the streets. I was sleeping in my car, living from post to post, my friends sneaking me into their rooms through windows to spend the night, a silent conspirator in my self-inflicted exile. I was actually living on the street, embracing a stark, dangerous reality.

After weeks and months went by, I started getting used to the streets, learning their brutal, unforgiving ways. I'd be out until three or four in the morning, entangled in the nocturnal rhythms of that life, and still try to drag myself to school, a fleeting nod to a life I was rapidly abandoning. Out there, I met all kinds of different characters—people I would have never seen in my sheltered middle-class life, figures from the shadows. I saw things that were crazy, violent, and profoundly disturbing, learning all this at a tragically young age, absorbing the dark lessons of survival. The things I saw and went through started turning me into an animal, hardening my heart, dulling my empathy. I was meeting hookers, drug dealers, hardened criminals—everyone and everything that represented a life far removed from my upbringing.

Next thing you know, I was fully immersed in this lifestyle, living it, breathing it, part of it. Older people, recognizing my raw potential and hunger, started taking me under their wing, showing me how to hustle in these streets, how to do this and that, initiating me into their twisted world. Soon, I was making money, a lot of money. I thought that was what it was all about—making money, getting fancy cars, flashy jewelry, all the superficial trappings of success.

That's the lifestyle I became dangerously addicted to, a seductive trap disguised as success—until it crushed me. But the fundamental problem is, that lifestyle was fool's gold, a glittering deception, because that's precisely what led me directly into the life sentence I eventually received. Trouble is easy to get into, so seductive in its immediate gratification, but it's brutally hard to get out of. And that's exactly what happened to me. When you play in the mud, expect to get dirty. It took me a long, painful while to learn that undeniable truth, which is precisely why self-reflection is so profoundly important, so utterly crucial. Self-reflection taught me, and it hurt me to realize it: you have to strip yourself down to your essence.

Even though I was so mad, blaming everything and everyone on the unfair sentence the judge gave me—which people can still agree was very harsh, a severe judgment—I finally broke everything down. I looked at myself with true, unsparing self-reflection and, for the first time, started holding myself accountable.

I realized, with a clarity that pierced through my years of denial, "Hey, you would never have been able to get that life sentence if you never went in front of that judge, if you never opened the doors to give him reason to give you that life sentence, if you never went to jail, if you never been doing illegal things out there to go to jail and be put in front of that judge." The chain of cause and effect became undeniably clear. I would never have gone to jail if I wasn't doing anything illegal, if I wasn't running in those treacherous streets, or hanging around with people who indulged in that type of bad activity, if I wasn't actively participating in that destructive lifestyle. It's like they say, "Birds of a feather flock together." And that's what came from that initial bad decision and irresponsible thinking when I walked out the house, packed my car, and went out there in the street. That one bad decision was like a domino effect, setting off a cascade of consequences that led directly to my downfall.

A lot of times, we don't realize these fundamental truths until we sit, strip ourselves down, and look at the raw truth behind our lives, or behind the critical decisions we've made, and see that it's all within yourself. You possess the power to get this done, to change your trajectory. That's why **RGD** is not external; it is within you, waiting to be unleashed. That will build you and allow you to be more accountable. Because when you have that profound accountability, it brings that vital knowledge to identify your issues, which is your indispensable first step to owning up to it. Then you learn from it, truly absorbing the lessons. Then, after that, you understand how to use it as an advantage, transforming weakness into strength.

It was in that desperate, relentless search for survival, for a way to preserve my sanity and my very self, that I stumbled upon the blueprint. It wasn't a sudden, blinding flash of light, but a slow, arduous, grinding realization, painstakingly forged in the relentless pressure and isolation of confinement.

I called it **RGD: Resilience, Growth Mindset, and Discipline**. These weren't abstract concepts from some dusty self-help book or philosophical treatise. These were visceral, lived principles I had to embody, to live, breathe, and bleed every single day just to survive, let alone endure. And they are the exact same principles that can transform any life, regardless of how dire the circumstances, how deep the hole.

Pillar 1: Resilience – The Art of Bouncing Forward

My time inside wasn't just about serving a sentence; it was a goddamn masterclass in forging resilience. let me tell you, that ain't some soft self-help buzzword in here; it's the raw, unyielding grit you find when every damn thing tries to break you, and you just spit in its eye and keep swinging. This wasn't about simply bouncing back to where you were; it was about bouncing forward, using the impact of adversity to propel you to a stronger, more evolved state. Take my appeals, for example—each one was a soul-crushing denial, over and over. The court basically sent me a "nope" in triplicate every few months, a constant reminder of the brick wall I faced. But I kept right on studying, kept filing, kept believing there was a way, even when the system seemed purpose-built to stomp out every flickering ember of hope.

Then came the gut-punch that damn near knocked me out of existence: my mother, Barbara Herring, gone, her unwavering light extinguished. Few years later, my father, another bedrock of my life, taken. And finally, my sister, Rrapanza, my steadfast champion, all while I was caged up, utterly unable to even say goodbye, to grieve properly, to be there for my family. That kind of pain—the triple blow of loss and helplessness—can bury a man. Snuff out his spirit completely. But instead, through a process of excruciating internal struggle, I found a way to transform that grief, that absolute wreckage, into something else, something sharper, something that fueled my resolve. And finally, when I walked out after **27 years**, I was a ghost in my own damn country because I was **"Tony Jackson"** on paper, without a single ID to prove I existed, a legal phantom... well, that was the final boss level, the ultimate test of my hard-won resilience.

But I tackled every bureaucratic nightmare, every dead-end phone call, every frustrating rejection, with the same relentless, bone-deep resilience I'd carved out in the belly of the beast. Turns out, when you've been to hell and back, proving you're actually a person with a birth certificate and a social security number is just another Tuesday. That's how you don't just survive; that's how you rewrite the whole damn script, transforming impossible obstacles into new pathways.

While some people may appear to be naturally more resilient, perhaps due to early experiences or temperament. But the truth? It's built. Day by day. it's generally understood as a dynamic process involving behaviors, thoughts, and actions that can be learned and developed over time, not a fixed personality trait. Resilience isn't just about surviving a tough time; it's about positive adaptation. This means maintaining or regaining healthy mental and physical functioning despite adversity, and often growing or finding new strengths and insights as a direct result of overcoming hardship.

Resilient individuals are better equipped to cope with both everyday stressors and major, life-altering challenges. They possess effective coping strategies that help them manage their emotions, thoughts, and behaviors in difficult, high-pressure situations, navigating the storm rather than being swept away.

A key aspect of resilience is being flexible and adaptable when faced with change or unexpected difficulties. This involves adjusting plans, thinking creatively to find new solutions, and finding innovative ways to approach problems when the old methods fail. Resilient people are skilled at recognizing and managing their emotions, practicing what is known as emotional regulation. They don't let negative emotions overwhelm them, but rather acknowledge them, allow themselves to feel them, and then find healthy, constructive ways to process and express them. Mistakes and setbacks are viewed not as devastating failures that define them, but as invaluable opportunities for learning from experience.

Resilient individuals reflect on what happened without judgment, analyze the situation, and use that hard-won knowledge to improve their future responses and strategies. It's crucial to understand that resilience doesn't mean "toughing it out alone," isolated and suffering. In fact, a significant component of true resilience is the ability to seek and effectively utilize social support from friends, family, and community, understanding that asking for help is a strength, not a weakness. Resilient individuals often maintain an optimistic outlook, even in the face of profound adversity. They can maintain a sense of perspective and hope, focusing on what they can control and believing, deep in their bones, in a positive future, even when it seems impossible.

Here's a little something to chew on: Life hits hard. Sometimes it feels like you're the punching bag in a hurricane, battered and broken. But real **resilience**? It's when you realize you're not the punching bag; you're the wind-up toy that just keeps wobbling back upright, no matter how many times it gets knocked down, even when you've lost an eye and a wheel. And sometimes, you just gotta laugh at the sheer absurdity of still standing, still fighting, still moving forward. That's when you know you've got something unbreakable in you"

How to cultivate Resilience:

Resilience isn't a trait you're born with; it's a muscle you build through consistent effort and mindful practice. Start by acknowledging adversity, not denying it or running from it. Then, analyze what happened, learn from it, and adapt your approach. Don't just pick yourself up; actively ask yourself how you can come back stronger, smarter, and with a clearer vision than before. It's about finding purpose in the pain, harnessing your inner strength, wisely utilizing all available resources, and proactively developing skills that enable a person to navigate life's inevitable challenges, recover rapidly from setbacks, and relentlessly continue to thrive, always bouncing forward.

Pillar 2: Growth Mindset – The Uncaged Mind

Here's the real kicker, the secret sauce to not just surviving that concrete jungle, but actually thriving, transforming even the most oppressive environment into a catalyst for self-improvement: I had to ditch the **"woe is me"** routine, that victim mentality, and wholeheartedly step into the arena of a **Growth Mindset**.

Turns out, staying pissed off and blaming everyone else for my life sentence—especially the one I wasn't even fully responsible for, the one I felt was grossly unfair— was as useful as yelling at a brick wall.

My mom, Barbara Herring, God bless her relentless heart, had been preaching accountability for years, planting those seeds of truth. "Pop," she'd tell me, her voice cutting through my self-pity, "you're in this mess because of you." It took about twenty trips to solitary, my personal little time-out spot, and countless internal battles for that profound wisdom to finally chip through my thick skull. I was staring down forever, an endless sentence, and the crushing realization dawned: my anger wasn't a weapon; it was just another chain binding me tighter to my misery.

So, I traded the rage for books, swapped pointless arguments for actual arguments in self-improvement classes, exchanging fury for focused learning. I wasn't just doing time anymore; I was enrolling in the School of Hard Knocks, curriculum: Advanced Self-Correction. Who knew I'd find my calling operating complex **CNC** machines and designing intricate furniture with **CAD** software? I was learning G-codes, man, an entirely new language of precision and creation, things I never knew existed, much less cared about in my street life.

It was like I tapped into a whole different brain, discovering latent abilities I never knew I had beyond, you know, surviving street brawls and navigating illicit deals. Turns out, when you truly put your mind to something, when you commit to continuous learning and improvement, even in a place designed to crush your spirit and limit your potential, you can do almost anything. It's not about being the smartest guy in the room; it's about being the one who's willing to learn when everyone else has given up, the one who sees potential where others see only limitation. And that, my friend, was my first real, undeniable taste of growth, the unlocking of my uncaged mind.

Unlike a **"fixed mindset"** (where people believe their talents, intelligence, and abilities are innate and unchangeable, set in stone from birth), a growth mindset sees intelligence and abilities as something that can expand and develop over time, much like a muscle that gets stronger with consistent exercise. People with a growth mindset view challenges and setbacks not as insurmountable obstacles or definitive signs of inadequacy, but as invaluable opportunities to learn, grow, and build new skills, viewing them as stepping stones rather than roadblocks. They understand that effort and persistence are crucial for genuine growth and lasting success. They don't give up easily when faced with difficulty; instead, they persist, try different strategies, and adapt their approach until they find a solution.

Mistakes are seen as valuable learning opportunities, not as embarrassing failures to be hidden or feared. They reflect on what went wrong with an analytical, non-judgmental eye, and use that knowledge to improve their performance and understanding. Individuals with a growth mindset are genuinely open to constructive criticism and actively seek feedback, viewing it as a powerful tool for improvement rather than a personal attack or a sign of weakness. They are inspired by the success of others and see it as motivation for their own growth, rather than feeling threatened or discouraged by someone else's achievements.

A key aspect of this mindset is using the transformative word "yet". For example, instead of saying "I can't do this," they say "I can't do this yet," which inherently implies that with continued effort, learning, and persistence, they will eventually be able to.

Adopting a **growth mindset** can lead to numerous profound benefits, including: increased **resilience** and ability to bounce back more quickly from setbacks; greater motivation and ambition, driving them to achieve more; enhanced problem-solving skills and creativity, finding innovative solutions; improved self-esteem and reduced stress/anxiety, fostering inner peace; a genuine love of learning and a deep commitment to lifelong development; and consistently better performance in both academic and professional settings.

Let's break it down: Think of life like a brutally difficult video game. When you hit a 'Game Over' screen, do you throw the controller in frustration and declare yourself a permanent loser, abandoning the game forever? Or do you take a deep breath, restart, knowing exactly where that monster jumps, or which button combo you messed up, ready to try again with new insight?

A **growth mindset** is seeing every **'defeat'** as a vital clue, an essential piece of information for the next attempt. It's not 'I can't beat this level.' It's 'I haven't found the right strategy...

yet.' So go ahead, get knocked down. Just hit 'retry' with a defiant grin, because you're one critical step closer to figuring out the cheat code for your own damn victory.

My story isn't just about surviving; it's a living, breathing testament to the raw, transformative power of a **growth mindset**. It's the simple, yet revolutionary, understanding that your brain isn't some rigid, finished product, but a dynamic, malleable muscle that gets stronger, smarter, and more capable with every challenge, every mistake, every single ounce of effort you pour into it. When life slammed me with a **"life"** sentence, stripped me of my identity, and ripped away the people I loved most, a fixed mindset would've just thrown in the towel, convinced I was doomed, that my fate was sealed. But that's not how we play.

How to cultivate a Growth Mindset:

So how do you build a **Growth Mindset**? Start here: see every wall as a ladder. Every setback? A lesson in disguise. Every stumble? A step forward, every failure as data. Trade debilitating rage for the quiet, grueling work of learning— not just from books, but from every stumble, every unexpected victory, every interaction. Actively unearth talents you never knew you possessed, proving to yourself that when you truly believe your potential is limitless, you start reaching for things you once thought impossible. It's the undeniable proof that when you cultivate a growth mindset, you unlock a relentless drive to adapt, to persist, to continuously improve, and to truly live up to your highest goals, no matter how daunting the starting line appears.

Pillar 3: Discipline – The Architect of Progress

If a **growth mindset** is the belief system, the unshakable conviction that you can learn and grow, then then **discipline** is the daily grind that makes it real—the gritty, no-excuses, the consistent, unglamorous effort that turns that belief into cold, hard reality. In a place like prison, where every fiber of your being screams rebellion, where external control is absolute, choosing self-discipline felt like tying my own damn shoelaces together with barbed wire—an act of profound, voluntary restraint. It wasn't about the guards forcing me; it was about me forcing myself, imposing my own will. My inner hothead, the one who wanted to curse out every official within earshot, had to learn to sit down and shut up while my newfound discipline told me to hit the books instead, to channel that rebellious energy into something constructive.

I was studying law until my eyes blurred, poring over statutes and case law, even after the tenth, twentieth appeal denial, each one a crushing blow. That wasn't fun; it was a conscious, brutal choice to apply myself to something bigger than my immediate rage, something that promised a distant, elusive freedom.

This wasn't some flashy, movie-montage heroic act; it was the boring, consistent work that piled up, day after day, week after week. It was the hours I spent meticulously learning **CNC** programming and **CAD** design, complex skills that felt light-years away from the street chaos I'd known. Who knew I'd find my peace programming a machine to carve wood, transforming raw material into something beautiful and functional?

This was **discipline** in action: showing up, focusing, and persisting. Then, walking out of prison with literally nothing but the clothes on my back and a mountain of bureaucratic hell to climb, **discipline** became my GPS, my unwavering guide. It was showing up every single damn day to fight for my identity, navigating foreign birth certificates, long-gone German hospitals, and indifferent government agencies.

Discipline taught me that absolute freedom isn't just about unlocking a gate; it's about unlocking your own potential through consistent, unsexy effort, even when every part of you and go eat a donut and forget the entire ordeal. Turns out, the "**magic**" people talk about, the seemingly effortless success, the monumental achievements? It's usually just discipline showing up for work, day after day, until the impossible becomes undeniable, until the dream becomes a tangible reality.

At its core, **discipline**, especially "**self-discipline**," is the ability to control one's impulses, desires, emotions, and behaviors in pursuit of a greater goal. It's about foregoing immediate gratification in favor of long-term objectives, understanding that present sacrifice yields future reward. This involves actively regulating your thoughts and actions to stay on track, to adhere to your chosen path.

Discipline is the crucial bridge between fleeting goals and tangible accomplishment. It's the consistent application of effort and unwavering adherence to a plan, even when it's difficult, boring, or unappealing, to move consistently closer to your objectives. It's about taking small, consistent steps of daily action, understanding that incremental progress builds monumental change.

Discipline is closely linked to the powerful formation of good habits. By repeatedly performing desired actions, even when motivation wanes, those actions eventually become ingrained as habits, requiring less conscious effort and becoming automatic behaviors. A disciplined individual is inherently persistent and persevering. They don't give up easily in the face of obstacles, setbacks, or a frustrating lack of immediate results. They learn from mistakes, adjust their strategies, and continue to work relentlessly towards their goals.

Discipline often involves creating order and structure in one's life. This can include setting routines, prioritizing tasks, managing time effectively, and eliminating distractions that pull you off course. The word "discipline" itself comes from the Latin word **"discipulus,"** meaning "**pupil,**" or "**learner**," and "**disciplina**," meaning "teaching" or "instruction." In this sense, discipline is about teaching oneself or others to follow a particular code of conduct or to develop a skill, a continuous process of self-instruction and refinement. This can also extend to "**child discipline**," which focuses on teaching children appropriate behaviors and boundaries.

It's important to distinguish **discipline** from motivation, as they are often confused. Motivation is often the initial emotional drive or fleeting inspiration to start something, that burst of enthusiasm. However, when that initial motivation inevitably wavers, when the excitement fades, it is **discipline** that enables you to continue despite your emotions and thoughts, despite your urges to quit. **Discipline** acts as the steadfast force that keeps you moving forward even when you don't feel like it, even when every fiber of your being screams to stop.

Here's a little something to chew on: **Discipline** is like flossing your teeth. Nobody wakes up screaming with joy, "Woohoo! Time to floss!" It's boring, repetitive, and often gets skipped in favor of easier, more gratifying activities. But ignore it long enough, and you're looking at a world of pain and expensive dental bills. Keep at it, however, for just a few minutes a day, and you've got a sparkling smile and healthy gums. It's the small, consistent, often unglamorous things you do daily that prevent the big catastrophes and build the jaw-dropping results. So go on, floss your life; choose the consistent, seemingly small actions that will lead to massive, positive change.

Examples of **Discipline** in various aspects of life, illustrating its pervasive power. I saw each of these forms of **discipline** play out—not just behind bars, but in everyday life. Here's how **discipline** shapes every area:

- **Academic Discipline:** Consistent study habits, meeting deadlines, active listening, and focused attention in class, even when bored.
- **Physical Discipline:** Adhering strictly to a workout routine, maintaining a balanced, nutritious diet, and prioritizing adequate rest and recovery.
- **Financial Discipline:** Rigorous budgeting, consistent saving, and actively avoiding unnecessary debt to achieve long-term financial goals and security.
- **Professional Discipline:** Punctuality, effective task prioritization, meticulous organization, and a commitment to continuous professional development and skill acquisition.
- **Mental/Emotional Discipline:** Managing impulses, responding thoughtfully rather than reacting impulsively to challenging situations, practicing mindfulness, and cultivating a positive internal dialogue.

How to Cultivate Discipline:

Discipline is not a punishment; it is the ultimate act of self-love and self-respect. It is the consistent effort and self-control that allows individuals to overcome challenges, build positive habits, and ultimately achieve their desired outcomes and a more fulfilling life. Start small. Identify one single area where you want to improve and commit to consistent action, even for just 15 minutes a day.

Build habits by making those actions non-negotiable routines. Embrace discomfort as a clear sign of growth, a signal that you're pushing past your old limits. Understand that discipline isn't about restriction; it's about freedom—the profound freedom that comes from achieving your goals, mastering yourself, and living a life of true purpose and intentionality. It's not about doing what you feel like doing; it's about doing what you know you need to do, consistently, relentlessly, until it becomes second nature.

This is the power of **RGD**. It fundamentally changed my mentality and my very perception of what was possible, and it can change yours too. It's not about luck; it's about putting yourself in a position for these things to happen, regardless of your past, your present circumstances, or the obstacles that stand before you. That's when the true magic unfolds, and you finally live up to your full, immeasurable potential in life.

CHAPTER 3

THE UNBREAKABLE MIND – FORGING A MENTALITY OF STEEL

L et's cut the crap. You've seen the wreckage of my past. You've heard about the hothead who cursed out judges and stared down prison guards like it was just another Tuesday. But beneath that bravado? A world of pain—losing my mother, father, and sister, all while locked away, powerless to even say goodbye. And you've heard about the ghost of **"Tony Jackson,"** who walked out of prison after **27 years** with nothing but the clothes on his back and a bureaucratic nightmare ahead, a man erased by the system. So, how the hell did I go from that to standing here today, not just surviving, but actually thriving? The answer isn't luck. It's the relentless, painstaking, often brutally honest work of forging an unbreakable mentality.

This isn't some fluffy self-help jargon, some feel-good philosophy you can read on a greeting card. This is the steel-reinforced core I built, brick by painful brick, using the very elements that transformed my life: **Resilience, Growth**

Mindset, and Discipline (RGD). Think of it as your personal operating system. Most folks are running on a glitchy, error-prone version, programmed by fear, doubt, and external circumstances. But you? You're about to get the upgrade, the foundational code for true self-mastery.

This chapter isn't just about what I did; it's about how I thought, how I reshaped my beliefs, and how I systematically reprogrammed my own damn brain to navigate hell and come out stronger on the other side. Because your mind isn't just a part of you; it's the cockpit of your entire existence. And if you don't take deliberate, conscious control of the stick, life's inevitable turbulence will send you crashing.

No More Blame, No More Excuses: The First Weld of RGD

For years, I lived in a world where blame was currency, where externalizing fault was my go-to defense mechanism. You screwed up? Find a scapegoat. The system, the streets, my upbringing, bad luck, the dude who snitched, the judge who sentenced me – the list was endless, a perpetual scroll of external culprits. I was a master craftsman of excuses, building elaborate mental fortresses to protect myself from the uncomfortable, searing reality that I was the common denominator in all my misfortunes. It was always someone else's fault, someone else's decision, someone else's limitations holding me back. And let me tell you, living like that? It's a prison on its own. A self-made cage, arguably even worse than the concrete walls I eventually found myself behind, because it was a cage of my own design, built from self-deception.

This toxic mindset was the absolute antithesis of the Growth Mindset I desperately needed to cultivate. It shut down any possibility of accountability, which is the bedrock of all true progress and transformation.

Why do we play the blame game? Simple. Because It's deceptively comfortable. It feels good for a second, maybe, a fleeting reprieve from self-reflection. It absolves us of responsibility, of the heavy burden of consequence. If it's someone else's fault, then we don't have to change, we don't have to admit we messed up, and we don't have to face the uncomfortable truth that we're the only ones truly in control of our responses, our reactions, our internal world. It's a psychological shield, paper-thin but deceptively strong, protecting our fragile ego from the hard reality of our own choices.

But that comfort? It's a lie. It's a slow poison that paralyzes you, keeps you shackled. When you point the finger, you don't just assign blame; you give away your power. You become a perpetual victim, trapped in circumstances you believe are entirely beyond your control. And trust me, I was a grand champion of the blame game for a long, long time. Every day was a fresh opportunity to cast myself as the aggrieved party, to rail against the unfairness of it all.

Think about it. We see this insidious pattern everywhere, right?

- **The "My Job Sucks" Trap:** "I'd be successful if my boss wasn't a micromanager." "I'd be making more money if this company just valued its employees." The job might genuinely have issues, sure, but how many people use that as an excuse to stop learning, stop networking, stop actively seeking new opportunities? They blame the job instead of diligently building skills to get a better job or even create their own. Their success isn't out of their hands; it's out of their sustained effort.

- **The "Financial Chains" Trap:** "I can't save money because the economy is terrible." "I'm always broke because life is too expensive." Yes, financial realities are tough, and the system can be rigged. But how many take the hard, honest look at their own spending habits? How many commit to learning about budgeting, investing, or generating additional income streams? They blame the market, not the choices they make with their dollar, however small.

- **The "Relationship Rollercoaster" Trap:** "My relationship is always messy because my partner is so difficult." "I can't find love because everyone out there is crazy." Sure, other people undeniably contribute to relationship dynamics. But are you examining your communication style? Your emotional triggers? Your own recurring patterns of attracting certain types of people or repeating the same destructive dances? Blaming the "other person" ensures you repeat the same damn cycle forever; stuck on a ride you despise.

Every single one of these blame traps is a choice—a decision to stay stuck, to remain impotent. It's a refusal to look in the mirror, to assume agency. It's living with a heavy invisible chain, even if you're physically free, because your mind is enslaved. The true, devastating consequence of blame isn't just a missed opportunity; it's the insidious erosion of your own power, the slow draining of your vital life force. It builds resentment, limits your vision to only what's wrong, and keeps you from ever identifying the real levers of change—which are always, always within you, within your sphere of influence.

This initial, foundational step of shedding blame is absolutely critical for cultivating Resilience and Discipline, as you simply cannot adapt, grow, or consistently work towards improvement if you are always looking outward for fault, always pointing fingers.

It took me a long, agonizing time, and a whole lot of internal screaming and struggle, to finally walk away from that blame filled life. The true turning point wasn't some sudden external freedom, some magical key from the outside; it was the brutal self-analysis, that moment of finally looking in the mirror and saying, with gut-wrenching honesty, "Okay. My choices put me here. My mentality kept me here. It's on me."

And let me tell you, that realization? It wasn't depressing. It wasn't soul-crushing. It was the most liberating feeling I've ever known. It was like taking off a heavy, suffocating coat

I hadn't realized I was wearing for decades, suddenly able to breathe freely, to move unencumbered.

Why? Because if it's on you, then you're not a victim. You're the damn pilot of your own life. You're not subject to the whims of fate or the faults of others. You might not control the external storm, but you absolutely control your ship, your navigation, your response, and your destination. You control where you steer next. That simple, profound shift in perspective—from "Why did this happen to me?" to "What am I going to do about it?"—is the critical first step in building an unshakeable foundation for your mind. It's the ultimate act of self-empowerment. This profound shift in perspective is the very essence of the **Growth Mindset**.

Reprogramming the Cockpit: Attitude, Self-Talk, and Understanding the True Meaning of Strength

The real game-changer? It's not just about stopping the bad thoughts, the negative self-talk that constantly undermines you; it's about actively, systematically replacing them with something solid, something constructive. It's about cultivating positive self-talk that hits harder, more resilient, and more persuasive than your inner critic. When that insidious voice inside whispers, "You're a loser, you'll never get out, you're stuck forever," you learn to actively drown it out with, "I'm learning, I'm growing, I will find a way, no matter what." You start reframing those negative thoughts, not by denying their existence, but by dissecting their faulty logic and twisting them into fuel for your furnace of resolve.

That unfair sentence? My mind learned to reframe it into, "This is the ultimate test of my resourcefulness, my ingenuity, my spiritual fortitude." The profound pain of loss, of missing my mother, father, and sister? It became a burning reminder of who I was fighting for, a silent promise to make their sacrifices, their love, mean something, to honor their memory with my transformation.

This mental warfare—this daily fight to control the story in your head—was just as real, just as brutal, as any fight I ever faced on the streets or behind bars, and it's a battle you definitely win by choosing your thoughts, by directing your focus, not by letting them choose you. That is where mental discipline becomes paramount, enabling Resilience in the face of internal attacks and corrosive self-doubt.

Let me tell you about P-Man. He was a street legend, a no-nonsense dude who could snap in a second, a force to be reckoned with. People feared him, but he was also a well-known hustler, respected in that twisted ecosystem. We ended up in the same high-security prison, and we'd talk about old times, kick it, joke around, and share stories from our shared past. However, as I embarked on my journey, rigorously changing my mindset, I began to see a profound and tragic problem with P-Man. He was letting his mind control him, utterly consumed by its darkness. He'd done so much "dirt" in his past, and that same over-aggressive, street-hardened character, that deep-seated paranoia, was still deeply ingrained in him, eating away at him from the inside.

It got to the point where that character started devouring him, poisoning his every thought. Small disagreements would escalate wildly in his mind; if he saw two people talking who he'd had a past dispute with, he'd immediately jump to the conclusion that they were plotting on him, setting him up, or about to jump him. He'd come to me, his eyes burning with perceived injustice, saying, "Hey, Pop, we gotta go take somebody out," trying to recruit me to help him fight or attack someone because he truly, genuinely believed they were out to get him, to harm him. I'd try to understand, to intervene, thinking I could help keep him out of harm's way. Still, when we'd confront the individuals, it was almost always a misunderstanding, a misinterpretation, nothing.

Even if they apologized, his mind was still set on battle, irrevocably biased towards conflict. He just automatically thought in a negative, conspiratorial way, without any actual truth or evidence of what he was perceiving. His view of reality had become warped—like he couldn't see straight, couldn't trust what was real anymore; his logic didn't even make sense to me anymore. His inability to control his mind, to challenge those false narratives, those destructive assumptions, was a self-made trap that constantly pulled him deeper into peril, into a cycle of self-fulfilling prophecy. I tried to talk to him, to reason with him, to get him to calm down, explaining that his unbridled mentality was going to get me "f****d up" too. That's when I knew, with a heavy heart, that I had to pull myself away from him, to protect my own burgeoning sanity and progress.

Here's a little something to chew on: Your brain is a terrible master but an excellent servant. It'll wreck your life if you let it run the show—but trained right, it's your deadliest weapon. Too many people let their minds run wild, unchecked, like a toddler with a credit card in a candy store, indulging every whim and fear. But when you train it-when you deliberately, consistently make it serve your highest goals—it becomes your most powerful ally, your greatest asset. So, here's the real question: Are you the boss of your brain, or is your brain dragging you around by the nose like a confused poodle?

This principle of mind control, of actively governing my thoughts, truly changed my perspective on everything. For example, when I was learning **CAD** (Computer-Aided Design) and operating **CNC** (Computer Numerical Control) machines, I was part of a special prison vocational program that actually designed and produced high-end furniture for offices, libraries, and even hotels. It was crazy, right? Making sophisticated, valuable furniture from behind prison bars. The pay? A whopping 55 cents an hour, the absolute maximum you could earn in the prison system.

My homeboys, still trapped in the old mindset, would look at me like I was utterly insane. "Man, you're really working for 55 cents an hour?" they'd scoff, shaking their heads like I'd lost my mind. But back in the day, that dismissive attitude, that focus solely on immediate, insufficient gain, would have had me quitting on the spot, fueled by perceived insult.

However, with my new mentality, that profound shift in my **Growth Mindset**, it wasn't about the measly 55 cents. It was about knowledge. It was about education. I was getting paid—however little—to learn invaluable, marketable skills that people on the outside paid big money for, skills that were highly sought after. This wasn't just a job; it was my personal university, my efficient, hands-on school.

My mentality had shifted to seeing the bigger picture and looking at things in a more positive, forward-thinking way. That change in perspective, that new mental framework, allowed me to see the actual, lasting value in what I was doing, far beyond the paltry hourly wage. This embodies the very spirit of the Growth Mindset – finding profound opportunity and invaluable learning in unexpected places, prioritizing long-term growth and skill acquisition over immediate, fleeting gain.

From "King Kong" to Calm Conviction: The Power of Evolved Attitude

Before prison, and even during my early days inside, I carried an "I ain't nothing to be f****d with" attitude. It was a defiant posture, a constant readiness to attack, to be perpetually on the defensive, to "check somebody" and aggressively put them in their place. I didn't run from conflict; I actively sought it out, inviting it. I was King Kong in my jungle—loud, aggressive, always ready to throw down—the undisputed alpha. I always had that spark, that raw, untamed fire in me, a coiled spring of aggression.

I was skilled with my hands, having taken Taekwondo as a kid and boxing; I always had heart and never backed down from anything, no matter the odds. I was never a bully; I never started things without provocation. However, I was always ready when conflict came my way, and I would absolutely never de-escalate a situation. You picked a fight with me; you signed up for a long day. Or if I could impose my will quickly, it might be a short, brutal one.

This mentality, this aggressive readiness, felt like it protected me on the streets, a necessary shield in a brutal world. It molded me into that type of person, and prison only amplified it, raising that level of intensity even higher. However, as I genuinely and desperately wanted to change, to escape the self-destructive cycle, I had to realize that my aggressive attitude wasn't going to get me far in life if I truly wanted to elevate myself, to be a better person, and to be more open-minded and understanding. I had to make a complete about-face, a total reorientation of my approach to interaction. Being overly aggressive, like King Kong, doesn't gain you more respect in the long run. It doesn't make you bigger or more challenging than the next person; it just makes you feared, isolated, and constantly on edge.

I began studying other leaders, not just those in prison, but leaders throughout history in various fields. And I noticed something profound, something counterintuitive to my street logic: some of them had this remarkable calm demeanor, an almost quiet presence, yet their words were mighty, their influence undeniable. They spoke with profound respect and with genuine, unshakeable conviction. When they said, their words alone carried immense power, a gravitas that commanded attention. People truly listened, not out of fear, but out of genuine respect for their wisdom and composure. They accomplished far more with a calm, centered state of mind than someone would have ever achieved with a fist or threats. Many true leaders possess that quiet strength, that inner peace, and I realized I was doing it the hard way, the destructive way, for far too long.

This understanding, birthed from a deepening Growth Mindset, started teaching me a better way, a more effective path to power. It broadened my perspective, showing me that I didn't have to "gorilla" people or beat my chest to stand firm, to command respect. My true strength, my lasting influence, came not from physical intimidation but from understanding, from hard-won wisdom, and the unwavering conviction of my values and principles. It changed me from the inside out.

Now, I don't have to beat my chest like King Kong, but this evolved thinking allows me to respectfully speak to someone, explain myself clearly, and achieve a strong, mutual understanding, even in the face of disagreement. When you authentically give respect, you genuinely get respect. This was a profound, life-altering realization for me, and I began to understand how it made everything during my prison time, as well as my life outside, seem a lot easier, allowing for more open-mindedness, smoother interactions, and a greater sense of peace. This shift in attitude, requiring immense self-control and consistent effort, is a direct application of **Discipline** and a hallmark of a true **Growth Mindset**.

And let me be clear: that fire, that spark, that fundamental capacity for toughness and assertiveness? It's still there. It's part of my genetic makeup, a part of who I am, a raw, primal energy. And some people might try to blame their "genetic makeup" or their "temperament" for why they can't control themselves, why they constantly react instead of respond, but that's just another excuse, another surrender of power.

The **Growth Mindset** opens the door to self-mastery, enabling you to transcend your default settings. It allows you to take control, to reshape your mind, and to deliberately rethink and refocus on bettering yourself and evolving. It helps you understand precisely how to control that "beast" within, how to channel its energy productively. I had to learn how to control that beast and integrate it wisely. I wanted to be better, so I did everything I could to tuck it away, to put it in a safe, controlled place, to disarm its destructive potential.

I'm not saying I'm a pushover or that I don't still possess that power. I'm saying I have control of it now; it doesn't control me. It's no longer on the front line, leading every charge, because it doesn't accurately represent the evolved me. I'm the one who's in control of my actions, of what I do, of who I am. And that becomes real when your mindset shifts—into something more positive, more intentional.

The **Growth Mindset** can fundamentally change that mentality and make you a better person, putting you more in control of yourself, making you the person you truly want to be. It's all on you; you can't blame it on anything else. You have to keep control, have full control of that inner landscape, because you can always improve yourself. The

Growth Mindset will allow you to understand that you can always be better, always evolve.

Setting Goals, Celebrating Wins, and Choosing Your Circle

Let's talk about setting goals, not wishful daydreams that leave you empty, but realistic, actionable goals that you can actually grab hold of and achieve. For years, "getting out" felt like a distant planet, an unattainable dream. So, I learned to break it down into smaller, manageable victories: learning **CAD**, mastering the CNC machine, getting that prestigious prison vocational job. Each skill learned, each small achievement, was a tangible victory, a step forward. And you know what happens when you stack those small victories, one on top of the other? Your confidence doesn't just grow— it gains momentum like a freight train.

Whether I nailed a G-code, led my team to a championship, or faced yet another appeal denial and walked away with a new insight about the law—it was all fuel, a concrete piece of proof that I was capable, that I was progressing. Don't let anyone, especially yourself, diminish those wins, no matter how small they seem to others. Savor them. Let them fuel your fire. They're not just marks on a scoreboard; they're the building blocks of an unshakeable belief in yourself. This relentless pursuit of smaller goals, even in the face of setbacks, showcases the power of Resilience and Discipline.

And here's another truth carved in stone; a lesson learned from the hard realities of the street and prison: you become who you hang around. In prison, that meant consciously, deliberately stepping away from the endless drama, the toxic bitterness, and the cycle of self-pity that can swallow you whole before you even notice.

On the outside, it means actively surrounding yourself with positive influences – people who uplift, who challenge you to be better, who genuinely believe in growth, not just misery and stagnation. Actively avoiding negative people or draining situations isn't a weakness; it's a smart, strategic act of self-preservation. It's protecting your hard-won mental peace, because a strong mentality is like a fortress; you don't invite saboteurs through the gates. This ain't about being judgmental; it's about being discerning. This is a crucial act of **Discipline** in safeguarding your **Growth Mindset.**

The Unbreakable Outcome

At the end of the day, cultivating this strong, solid mentality rooted in **Resilience, Growth Mindset, and Discipline**—powered by deliberate positive self-talk and surrounded by supportive forces—isn't just for getting through hell. It's for building heaven right here on Earth, for creating the life you genuinely desire. It leads directly to making better decisions, the kind that steer your life with purpose, not just wherever the wind blows you-or old habits-try to take you   It cultivates improved relationships, because you're operating from a place of strength, clarity, and self-awareness, not reactivity or fear. And in the end, it's the direct path to greater overall happiness, a profound sense of peace, unwavering purpose, and true fulfillment.

Your mind is your greatest asset; learn to command it, learn to forge it into steel, and there's no hardship you can't conquer, no goal you can't reach, no version of yourself you can't become. Trust me - I'm living proof.

CHAPTER 4

ADVERSITY – THE GRINDSTONE OF GREATNESS

L et's get one thing straight, right now - adversity isn't a maybe. It's not an optional experience you can dodge. It's not some monster under your bed that might show up if you're unlucky enough. Adversity is inevitable. It's the sudden, unexpected rain on your parade, the wrench jamming your well-oiled gears, the brutal, unexpected punch to the gut that deals with everyone, rich or poor, saint or sinner. You can run from it, you can deny its existence, you can even curse its name with every fiber of your being, but you cannot escape it, no matter what you do.

It's a fundamental, unavoidable part of the human experience, as constant and undeniable as the sunrise. The only choice you get is how you face it, how you respond when it inevitably knocks on your door, and how you move through the storm and emerge stronger, sharper, and more resilient.

On the other side, is precisely where **Resilience, Growth Mindset, and Discipline (RGD)** become your indispensable allies, your battle-tested armor. This isn't just about my story, though it's deeply woven into every fiber of it; it's about how **RGD** offers a proven blueprint for anyone to navigate the inevitable challenges life throws their way and master their mentality in the process, transforming obstacles into opportunities.

My life? A relentless, unforgiving masterclass in getting intimately acquainted with adversity. From the reckless, dangerous ballet of the streets, where every dark corner held a potential ambush or a life-altering choice, to the screaming, chaotic flight deck of a warship—where the deafening roar of jet engines and a single wrong step meant oblivion—and then into the concrete maw of a cold, impersonal prison cell, adversity was my constant, uninvited companion.

I had to grow up fast, learning to read the room and adapt on the fly with lightning speed, whether navigating rival crews and volatile situations or dodging a jet wash that almost blew me into the churning ocean. Even after I walked out—a free man, yet a legal ghost—stripped of identity, recognition, and any proof I'd ever existed, the hits kept coming. No ID, no birth certificate, no evidence of existence, just another formidable mountain to climb, another layer of soul-crushing bureaucratic absurdity to hack through. Every step of that journey was adversity, relentless and unforgiving.

When I was in prison, immersed in that concentrated crucible of hardship, adversity didn't just visit—it flooded every damn day. It was far from the best time of my life, a period of immense struggle. Initially, I didn't know how to deal with it; I kept "crashing out"— snapping under pressure, losing my mind, banging my head against the wall like that would fix something, letting my raw emotions take over and dictate my destructive reactions. Too many times, I handled adversity poorly, reacting with anger and frustration rather than thoughtful strategy. But slowly—painstakingly—I got better. I studied, I observed, I learned. And with each lesson, I grew - I followed the consequences of my unchecked responses.

Understanding **Resilience**, embracing a **Growth Mindset**, and rigorously applying **Discipline**—these were the transformative keys. Through what I was learning and experiencing, I began to navigate the dark times and even darker days with a newfound inner compass. And it's true: every challenge faced with this new framework kept making me stronger, better, and more capable. I genuinely felt like I was ready for the world, like Superman himself, prepared to take on anything when I finally got out.

But hell, even on the outside, adversity didn't quit. It just changed shape. That's when I truly realized that adversity isn't a temporary state; it's always present. You will always be in a continuous cycle of learning, adjusting, adapting, and growing to meet the ever-changing demands of the world. That's just how life is designed.

That profound realization made me truly feel like I had to embrace it, not fight it. And now, when I see adversity looming, I don't dread it; I smile. Especially now—when I've earned every damn reason to smile after crawling through the fire. So, when I face adversity now, it's no longer a big deal that overwhelms me. It's only a big deal if I make it one, if I choose to let it consume my mental peace. Instead, I see it as a learned lesson, an opportunity to test my forged steel.

Pain is Inevitable, Suffering is Optional: The RGD Instruction Manual

Here's a truth that hit me deep in my bones while I was picking up my life back together, a truth often attributed to wise men and ancient philosophies: "Pain is inevitable. Suffering is optional." That ain't just some feel-good quote for a motivational poster you tack on your wall. It's more than a quote— It's the damn instruction manual for navigating reality, for truly mastering your internal world. Adversity—the "pain" of life's inevitable curveballs, the blows you can't dodge—will always find you. It's a guaranteed part of the package deal, baked into the very fabric of existence. But how you respond to it, how you allow it to settle in your spirit, whether you choose to let it consume you in endless, crippling "suffering"—that's where your power lies, your ultimate freedom. And that's precisely where **RGD** steps in, giving you the tools to make that choice.

Resilience gives you the sheer grit and mental fortitude to absorb the blow and stand back up, unbroken, even when you feel shattered. A **Growth Mindset** helps you find the profound lesson in loss, the hidden wisdom in the wound, transforming raw Pain into an invaluable experience. **Discipline** is the consistent, unwavering action that keeps you moving forward, keeps you rebuilding, even when every fiber of your being screams for you to quit, to succumb to despair. That's the "optional" part of suffering—your ability to choose not to remain its victim.

Let this sink in until it becomes second nature: Adversity isn't just something you survive—it's something you need. Think about it. How the hell would you ever know how strong you truly are if you never had to pick yourself up off the canvas after being knocked down? How would you genuinely know your Resilience if you never faced a situation that tried, with every ounce of its might, to break you, to shatter your spirit? If you shelter a person, try to hide them from every bump and bruise, every disappointment—which, in a real sense, is an impossible and ultimately damaging endeavor anyway—you're not making them stronger. You're inadvertently setting them up for a catastrophic fall, just like the first-time life comes swinging with no warning. You're leaving them fragile, unprepared, mentally stuck in a place where real-world problems feel like unsolvable puzzles, where they don't know their damn strength because they've never had to tap into it, never been forced to dig deep.

Adversity is the forge. It's the roaring fire that hardens your steel, the brutal grindstone that sharpens your edge until it can cut through anything. It's not just beneficial; it's essential for survival, for becoming wiser, for becoming undeniably better than you were before. It's in the crucible of adversity that the principles of RGD are not just understood intellectually, but truly forged, tempered, and made unbreakable, transforming from theory into tangible, lived power.

So, if you're out there, locked in your war, and hearing that voice inside crying, 'Why me? Why this? Why now? "What if the very thing trying to break you is the only thing that can genuinely make you?

Sometimes, we intentionally choose paths that we know will be challenging because we understand they will lead to growth. This is a deliberate act of creating adversity for a beneficial outcome, a conscious decision to lift heavier weights. Additionally, we often make our adversity through our choices, actions, and mindset, sometimes without even realizing it, blinded by impulse, pride, or a lack of foresight. This is not about blaming yourself for past mistakes, but about understanding the profound and undeniable link between cause and effect. It's about recognizing the agency you always possessed, even when you didn't know how to wield it.

So, while we often face external adversity that's entirely beyond our control (like a war, or someone else's malicious actions leading to an unjust sentence, or the devastating, irreversible loss of loved ones), we also play a significant, often overlooked role in creating, prolonging, or choosing the adversity in our lives. Understanding this crucial distinction is key as it reveals exactly where you truly have power and agency and where **RGD** offers you the precise tools to wield that power effectively, turning self-inflicted wounds into powerful lessons.

Let me break bread and allow you to chew on this: Have you ever watched someone try to get strong in the gym? They don't just lift feathers, right? They pile on the heavy plates, straining, sweating, sometimes even letting out a grunt so guttural, it makes you wonder if they're lifting weights or trying to birth a small piano. Why? Because resistance builds muscle. Without the opposition, there's no growth. Adversity is life's heavy plate. It's the only way your mental and emotional muscles get strong enough to lift the impossible, to carry burdens you once thought would crush you. So next time life loads up the bar, don't complain about the weight; get ready to grow, get prepared to prove you're stronger than you think.

The Arrogant Walk-Out: How a Lack of RGD Created My Adversity

Remember the "arrogant walk-out" from my mom's house that I mentioned in Chapter 2? That impulsive decision, fueled by a short-sighted desire for perceived freedom and a profound lack of accountability, was a prime example of me actively creating my adversity, setting a chain of devastating consequences in motion. I was a bright kid, fearless and capable, genuinely interested in science, telescopes, and education, with a mind that could grasp complex concepts. However, I lacked the **Discipline** to consistently work hard and establish myself academically when faced with boredom or difficulty. When I got bored or just didn't feel like trying, I'd quit. It meant nothing to me—my commitment was fleeting. I pursued instant gratification without looking further into the destructive path I was setting myself on, without any foresight into its long-term cost.

My actions were driven by raw impulse, without deep thought, lacking the very foresight and strategic planning that **RGD** helps cultivate. My undeveloped **Resilience** meant I was unprepared for the real struggles outside the comfort and safety of home, crippling me rather than equipping me. I had no insight, no understanding of the profound, long-term consequences of my choices, as I lived strictly in the present moment.

That arrogant walk-out, that defiant departure, threw me headfirst into the brutal reality of street life, forcing me to become comfortable with things a young kid should never see, never experience. Homelessness became my shadow: bouncing from couch to couch at friends' places, sneaking in and out of windows, sleeping at girlfriends' houses, or just hustling on the concrete for enough cash to eat, to scrounge up a cheap, transient motel room. It was a brutal education, a constant, dehumanizing grind just to exist, to survive another day. But then, a different, more seductive kind of lesson began. These street veterans, with their hardened eyes and weary wisdom, saw something in me: a raw hunger, an untamed intelligence —and they took me under their wing. They taught me the hustle—how to flip a dollar into ten, then twenty, then a hundred—pulling back the curtain on the illusion of quick riches.

Suddenly, the grind wasn't just about survival; it was about flash and swagger. I was pulling in real money, more than I'd ever imagined, enough to buy nice cars that gleamed under the Florida sun, enough to drip in fancy clothes and heavy gold chains. The clubs, the women, the endless nights of partying and drinking—it all seemed like life. It wasn't just good; it was glorious, intoxicating. I thought I had made it, truly, achieved ultimate freedom. Doing whatever I wanted, whenever I wanted, without any perceived limitations or consequences.

Every high-five, every bottle popped, every new piece of jewelry cemented the dangerous lie that this was freedom, that this was truly living. I was fooling myself—hooked on the sweet lies the streets were feeding me. It was all flash, but it was a trap. I was setting myself up for a monumental, inevitable fall. My undeveloped **RGD**, my youthful lack of a truly unbreakable mentality, left me vulnerable to this kind of self-created adversity, a consequence of my own unexamined choices. Because the street life always, always catches up. And when it does, it doesn't ask politely. It demands a price, a steep one, for those fleeting "good times" you thought you were living. And trust me, I paid every single damn cent, and then some, with years of my life.

The Controlled Fire: Harnessing Your Inherent Strength

In Chapter 3, I discussed transforming my **"King Kong"** mentality, shifting from a brute force approach to one of calm conviction and deliberate power. It's critically important to understand that the fire, that primal spark, that inherent capacity for toughness and assertiveness, is still within me. It's part of my genetic makeup, a part of who I am, a force that can be used for good or ill. While some might try to blame their "genetics" or their "temperament" for why they can't control themselves, why they continually succumb to anger or impulse, that's just another excuse, another surrender of your agency.

The **Growth Mindset** allows you to take control. It's the key to reshaping your mind, to deliberately rethinking and refocusing on bettering yourself, on evolving past your raw instincts. I had to learn precisely how to control that beast within me, how to channel its immense energy. I wanted to be better, to transcend my past, so I did everything I could to secure it, to tuck it away safely, to master it. I might have put that aggressive nature in a safe, locked place, but I didn't throw away the key. Now, I carry that key. I'm in control of that beast, choosing when—or if—it needs to be let out, for what purpose, and with what measure of restraint. That choice? It's always mine.

My inherent power is no longer on the front line, dictating my actions through uncontrolled rage; it's a strategic force I now command, a disciplined tool in my arsenal. This conscious command over my inherent fire, transforming it from a liability into an asset, is a profound testament to applied **Discipline**, turning potential internal adversity into a harnessed strength that aids in overcoming any external challenge.

My Brother's Blueprint: RGD from an Early Age

I often reflect on how I wish I'd had the **RGD** principles instilled in me from an early age, like my younger brother. He may not have tested as high academically as I did or achieved the same grades, often struggling with traditional schooling. Still, he possessed something crucial I lacked for so long: a much better grasp of **Resilience, Growth Mindset, and Discipline** from a remarkably young age. When he set his mind to something, he stuck with it, relentless, no matter how tough it got. He was disciplined enough to show up to school every day, no matter how tough the work became, or how much he preferred other activities; he diligently studied to improve, always seeking mastery. He was truly resilient in the face of academic hurdles, willing to grow mentally, and remarkably disciplined on his chosen path to success. That's why he's successful today, a testament to these principles.

I vividly remember when he started playing the saxophone at the age of 12. He just took a liking to it, a nascent passion, and over the years, through consistent and disciplined practice, he improved, his skill blossoming. Next thing you know, he was a key member of the school band, practicing hard almost every day, listening intently to Kenny G, Miles Davis, and other jazz greats, learning not just the notes, but the soul of their music.

In high school, his dedication and leadership propelled him to become a drum major. Then, his talent and relentless **Discipline** earned him a coveted spot playing saxophone for one of the most famous college marching bands in the nation: Florida A&M University's legendary "The Marching 100." That experience, far more than just music, helped shape him, teaching him structure, teamwork, and persistence, which carried him through college. He went on to earn a Master's degree in education, building a solid academic foundation. He then methodically advanced through the school system, from a dedicated teacher to an administration dean, to an assistant principal, and eventually, after years of diligent effort, to a principal. Not just any principal, but he won "Principal of the Year" for Orange County, a testament to his profound impact and unwavering commitment.

This didn't come from sheer luck or innate genius; it came from relentless hard work and a mature understanding and application of the **RGD** concept, even if he didn't call it that, even if he didn't have a formal name for it. He applied it. Lived it. Breathed it, helping him move forward, step by step, and become the remarkable man he is today, which I applaud with immense pride.

My arduous journey taught me it's never too late to adopt these principles. This **RGD** trinity was vital for my reset, my profound transformation. Now, I'm doing things, understanding things, and acknowledging things I only wish I had known back then — truths that would have saved me decades of struggle. But that's precisely the point: the mistakes we made, the painful lessons learned, we can reapply ourselves, relearn, re-educate, and fundamentally reset ourselves using the **RGD** concept. Adversity is the grindstone. But **RGD**? That's the hammer and anvil that shape the steel of your unbreakable mind.

CHAPTER 5

INTEGRITY – THE UNSEEN ARMOR

L et's talk about something many people love to preach, but few live by: Integrity. It ain't just about not lying to your mama, or keeping your word when it's easy and convenient. True integrity is about staying true to your values and principles —even when the world twists you in knots, when temptation sweet-talks you, or when the easy road looks like a superhighway to everything you want. It's the unseen armor that protects your soul, the unshakeable bedrock beneath your feet that keeps you steady in any storm. And let me tell you, for a long time, my armor was made of Swiss cheese, useless and full of holes—and my foundation was nothing but shifting quicksand.

Back in the day, especially on the streets, integrity was a joke, a weakness, a liability that would get you played. You lied, you hustled, you manipulated, you played the dirty game to survive and thrive. My very existence, for years, was built on a lie, a fundamental dishonesty with myself and the world. Remember "Tony Jackson," the ghost name the system slapped on me, stripping me of my identity —was a daily reminder that I wasn't even honest with my damn self, let alone anyone else.

The street life itself was a masterclass in moral gymnastics: smiling in faces you planned to rob, making promises you knew you'd break the second it was advantageous, chasing money and superficial glamour through rampant deception. I was a walking contradiction, believing I was free while my conscience was locked in a cage, rattling its bars every damn night, a prisoner within my mind. This deep-seated lack of integrity was a direct reflection of an undeveloped **Resilience**, a stubbornly **fixed mindset**, and a profound lack of **Discipline** to resist instant gratification and consider the devastating long-term consequences of my choices.

When things inevitably went south, when the house of cards began to tumble, who did I blame? Everyone but the fool was staring back at me in the mirror. That ain't integrity; that's self-deception dressed in gold, a hustle built on dust. The actual cost of that kind of living isn't just legal trouble or external consequences, such as prison time. It's the silent, insidious erosion of your soul. It's the constant, exhausting mental gymnastics of remembering which lie you told to whom, the tangled web of deceit. It's the gnawing fear of being exposed, of your fragile facade crumbling, and the internal rot that comes from knowing, deep down, that you're not living up to who you genuinely want to be, who you know you could be. That inner conflict, that profound incongruence between your actions and your authentic self, is a prison all its own, far more suffocating than any concrete walls.

In prison, it's all about the hustle, about finding a way to survive, to gain some semblance of control or comfort in an environment designed to strip you of both. Whether you're selling drugs, making **"buck"** (prison wine), selling stolen kitchen food, washing clothes, or sneaking in contraband, there are countless ways people hustle to survive the scarcity and boredom.

Many guys didn't receive money from their families, so they found creative, often illicit, ways to make their own. When I first came in, still steeped in my old street mentality, I was part of that life, drawn to it by habit and perceived necessity. I had a lot of my homeboys, whom I knew from the streets, inside. And a few of them were the **"big dogs"** on the compound, the ones with all the connections, the **"plugs"** who controlled the flow of illicit goods. It was easy for me to get my hands on things, and that immediate access easily enticed me to hustle, to continue living by the street code. I was still wild, still operating under the same unexamined rules that most prisoners did.

But as I started growing and learning, actively trying to better myself and forge that unbreakable mind, that's when I realized integrity wasn't just an abstract concept; it was something I had to hold onto —a non-negotiable anchor. I made a hard, definitive decision: I quit selling drugs. Even though there was a significant amount of money in it, easy money that could have paid for a better lawyer and helped my family, I refused. This was a line I would not, could not, cross. And to be clear, I can pat myself on the back for this, with absolute certainty: I never used drugs a single day while I was in prison. I also consciously threw away prison wine and alcohol, knowing it wasn't healthy, knowing it only clouded the very mind I was trying to sharpen.

My refusal to sell drugs came from a deeper understanding I gained about life, a profound shift in my **Growth Mindset**. I started to truly see how much it destroyed families, how it broke people down, body and soul, and I witnessed firsthand in prison how badly drugs were affecting some of the other inmates, even my friends, turning them into shadows of themselves. I didn't want to be a part of that destruction, not anymore, and I didn't like the weight of that hanging over

129

my head – the haunting thought that I was the person who supplied the drug that broke someone, or that I'd be doing the same damn thing on the streets when I got out. You hear people say, "Oh, I won't do that on the streets," but if you're dealing with it right now, if you're compromising your principles today, that toxic pattern will follow you, a shadow you can't outrun.

It took a lot of inner strength, a lot of **Discipline**, for me not to sell drugs, especially with my inside connection to the "plug," where I could've made a ludicrous amount of money that would have solved many of my immediate problems. However, I held onto my integrity. I refused, and I forced myself to think bigger, to think long-term, because that's not something I wanted in my future, not a part of the man I was building. If I kept selling in prison, what would realistically stop me from doing it when I got out? I didn't want to be hustling like that on the street anymore. So, I stuck to my guns and held on to that nascent integrity with fierce determination. That's where integrity truly took over, becoming the guiding principle.

There was nobody else to get in my way or stop me; I chose that path deliberately. Even some of my friends, the "plugs" themselves, looked at me as if I were crazy. "Man, you mean you're going to turn down all this money?" they'd ask, incredulous. And I'd say, "Yeah," with quiet conviction. I kept working my 55-cent-an-hour job, making literal pennies compared to the drug money, but every penny was clean, earned with honesty. That was a strong, undeniable sign of my internal change, and it earned me a lot of significant, lasting respect from some of my friends and partners. They knew I was a stand-up person who truly stood by my principles, not just talked about them.

I might hustle in other, legitimate ways, but drugs? That was where I drew the line, a boundary etched in stone. That was about my morals and principles, and with my integrity, I refused to compromise, no matter the temptation or the perceived cost. The sheer peace of mind I gained from that decision, knowing I wasn't contributing to the widespread destruction, was worth far more than any illicit money or temporary relief from financial pressure. That was true freedom.

Flaws, Intentions, and the Power of Your Actions

Let's get this straight—everyone makes mistakes, and everyone has flaws. Being human means being messy, imperfect, prone to screwups—it's just part of the deal. The real game isn't about striving for an impossible flawlessness; it's about understanding your flaws, acknowledging your mistakes without defensiveness, and committing with genuine **Discipline** to learn and grow from them. It's about becoming a better version of yourself, day by day, through consistent effort and a **Growth Mindset**.

Sometimes, we act with genuinely good intentions, trying to do what's right, but the outcome is still bad, and unintended negative consequences ripple out. You may genuinely want to help and offer support, but your actions unintentionally cause harm or are simply ineffective. That's a mistake, a miscalculation, not a moral failing that defines your character. The crucial part is your awareness – when you realize you've hurt someone, even if you didn't mean to, you take accountability, learn from it, and change your approach for next time. That's the core of an open-minded approach to your behavior and thinking, a key aspect of the **Growth Mindset**.

But then there's the other side of the coin, the genuinely "flawed" move. If you commit an action knowing it's wrong, knowing it will cause harm, knowing it goes against your stated values, that's fundamentally different. That's a move made with flawed intention—a conscious choice to betray your principles—and it carries a deeper, heavier weight on your soul. This is where your integrity is truly tested and either strengthened or eroded, because you're consciously choosing to act against your higher principles, against the man or woman you aspire to be.

This brings us to the fundamental, undeniable truth: Your actions are a reflection of who you are. It's that simple, that stark. Actions speak louder than words, every single time, without exception. Your true character is not revealed in what you believe, but in what you do.

- If you consistently tell lies, you are a liar.
- If you consistently steal, you are a thief.
- If you consistently back down from what's right, you are a coward.

Every action starts in your head—with a thought, a choice, you made a conscious choice to complete that action. This is why getting your mentality straight and building an unbreakable mind is so critically important. It's about aligning your thoughts, intentions, and actions with the person you truly want to be and the values you want to embody. When you're about to act, pause for a second and ask yourself: Why am I doing this? What's the real reason behind it? Does this align with my integrity?

And remember, integrity isn't just displayed on a grand stage where everyone can see, in moments of public triumph or tragedy. It's often forged behind the curtains, in the quiet, unobserved moments when no one is watching but you and your conscience. It's in those seemingly small, insignificant, everyday decisions that your true character is revealed and built, brick by brick. This internal consistency, this unwavering commitment to your principles, is powered by **Discipline**, enabling a **Growth Mindset** to continuously refine your actions and maintain **Resilience** when the easy wrong calls your name.

Rebuilding Trust: The Daily Deposits and The Unseen Brand

For someone who has made past ethical failings and operated with compromised integrity, rebuilding that integrity is a painstaking and ongoing process. It's never about one big gesture or some dramatic apology that wipes the slate clean; it's about countless daily deposits of honest action and principled choices. It means making the hard, honest choice, over and over again, consistently, until it becomes your default, your automatic response, your second nature.

You have to earn back trust, not just from the people you may have wronged or disappointed, but, most importantly, from yourself. You have to prove to yourself, through consistent, undeniable action, that you are reliable, that your word means something, that your actions genuinely reflect your deepest values and aspirations. Every single time you choose integrity, every small, honest act, you're not just making a moral choice; you're actively repairing and strengthening your unseen armor, fortifying your inner foundation.

I've always been a man who holds his integrity with fierce conviction—now more than ever. I realize how profoundly important it is, and it's something we must do, relentlessly, because even when you think no one's watching, they are— taking note, making judgments. If you're a person of integrity, if you consistently do the right thing, you don't have to worry about what others see. You don't have to worry about being portrayed wrongly if you're already doing the right thing, living authentically. Your truth becomes your shield.

The Unseen Brand: Protecting Your Name

Let me serve you something to chew on: When you have integrity, when your principles and morals are held high, you realize that's what you stand on, the immovable ground of your being. But there's something else powerfully and intrinsically attached to your integrity, your principles, and your morals - your name.

And I find it supremely wise to always, always protect your name. Look at your name not just as an identifier, but as your most valuable brand. Think of some of the top-notch brands you encounter in the world—it could be Gucci, or a major, respected corporation like Apple or Mercedes. These companies do whatever it takes—spending millions if needed—to protect their name and reputation. Even if they have to hire expensive lawyers or launch massive PR campaigns, they go to the limit to protect their name, brand identity, and legacy.

As for yourself, you should do the same. You should always want to protect your name with the same vigilance and ferocity. You should never want your name associated with just anything, anything that goes against your deeply held morals, your principles, or your integrity. When you start allowing your integrity, principles, and morals to be compromised or violated, or when you let those things slip away due to laziness or temptation, your name is no longer solid; it becomes tarnished, its value diminished.

You don't want people to say your name and their face twist up like they're eating a sour lemon. You want people to say your name and smile, associating it with reliability, honesty, and a positive impact. You want people to speak positively about you, to respect your character. You want people willing to vouch for you on something good or excellent, because your reputation precedes you in the best possible way. Protect your name. Stand behind it with conviction that never shakes. Make sure nobody, and nothing, violates your integrity, your morals, or your principles. Never let your name get dragged into nonsense—scams, shady deals, or anything that stains your integrity. This requires immense **Discipline** and a **Growth Mindset** that values long-term reputation over short-term gain.

Just think about it: if you aren't proud of it, or you can't hold your head up high for it, why would you let your name be attached to it? So, be profoundly careful about how your name is put out there, because, like I said, your morals, principles, and integrity are intrinsically, powerfully, inextricably attached to your name. They are the same.

The Everyday Battles for Your Unseen Armor

Integrity isn't just tested in grand, life-or-death situations, such as refusing to sell drugs in prison or making a significant business deal. It's shaped—or slowly worn down—in the quiet, ordinary moments of daily life. These small, seemingly insignificant choices are what strengthen or chip away at your unseen armor, depositing into or withdrawing from your character bank account.

Think about it:

- **The "Little White Lie" Trap:** Your friend asks if you like their new, questionable outfit. Do you give an insincere compliment to avoid awkwardness, to make them feel good with a lie, or do you gently pivot to honesty, perhaps focusing on what you do like, without being false or hurtful? Each "little white lie" you tell, even with seemingly good intentions, subtly tells your subconscious that you're okay with bending the truth, that convenience trumps authenticity.

- **The "Cutting Corners" Challenge:** You're at work, under pressure, with a looming deadline, and you see an easy way to finish a task faster by skipping a step you know is essential for quality, but nobody will explicitly notice. Do you take the shortcut, sacrificing quality for speed, or do you do the job right, with meticulous Discipline, even if it takes longer and adds to your stress? Every corner cut is a subtle compromise to your commitment to excellence, which is a fundamental facet of integrity.

- **The "Gossip Game":** Someone starts dishing juicy, mean-spirited dirt on a mutual acquaintance. Do you eagerly join in, adding your fuel to the fire of negativity, or do you politely but firmly steer the conversation away, refusing to participate in tearing someone else down behind their back? Engaging in gossip erodes your integrity by devaluing others, contributing to negativity, and eventually diminishing your character.

- **The "Unclaimed Extra Change":** The cashier gives you back too much money, a clear error in your favor. Do you pocket it, knowing they won't realize, a secret windfall, or do you point it out and return it, even if it feels inconvenient? This is a micro-test of your honesty when no one is watching, a direct measure of your internal compass.

Every single one of these choices, no matter how small, how seemingly insignificant, reinforces your unseen armor—or weakens it, bit by bit. The ripple effect of consistently choosing integrity is profound. When you consistently live by your principles, when your word is your bond, people instinctively trust you. Your reputation becomes your strongest currency. Opportunities open up because you're seen as reliable, honest, and truly accountable. Conversely, a pattern of small compromises undermines your relationships, even if no one ever calls you out. Limits your true potential, and most importantly, erodes your self-respect. That's the internal cost of incongruence—the heavy, nagging feeling that you're not truly aligned with your best self, even if the world sees you as "successful."

Picture your conscience like a bank account. Each shortcut or compromise is a withdrawal. Small at first, maybe, a few cents here, a few dollars there, but those withdrawals compound, accumulating a debt of self-respect. True integrity is knowing that the only way to build real wealth—

real peace, absolute freedom, real self-worth—is through consistent, disciplined deposits of honesty, principle, and ethical action. You might not see the explicit balance on a ledger, but your soul feels every single transaction, every withdrawal, every deposit.

And here's another piece for your mental plate: Think about the strongest buildings, the ones that stand for centuries, resisting earthquakes and hurricanes, or the most unshakeable bridges that bear immense loads. They aren't built on shaky ground or slapdash construction—they're anchored by solid foundations laid with care, often hidden from view, constructed with meticulous care and robust materials. Integrity is the foundation for your life. You can stack all the achievements, all the money, all the fame, all the accolades on top, but without integrity as your base, it's just a house of cards waiting for the next gust of wind to collapse it. What kind of structure are you truly building? A temporary facade or an enduring monument to your true self?

And the payoff? The freedom, my friend, the absolute, unshakeable freedom of a clear conscience. When your actions align perfectly with your values, when you're not constantly looking over your shoulder for the past to catch up, when you're not carrying the heavy weight of lies and regrets—that's a liberation that concrete walls and prison bars could never touch. It's a peace that no amount of street money or fleeting glamour could ever buy, a quiet confidence that radiates from within. Doing what's right isn't just a moral choice; it's the ultimate act of self-care, leading directly to better decisions, stronger, more authentic relationships, and a profound, lasting sense of inner peace and purpose. It's the unseen armor that truly protects you, not from the world's attacks, but from the most dangerous enemy of all: yourself.

So, I ask you: How does this represent you? What compromises are you making today that are quietly eroding your peace of mind, chipping away at your unseen armor? Are you truly free? Or are you just carrying a lighter set of chains, self-imposed and invisible?

CHAPTER 6

LUCK – THE OPPORTUNITY YOU EARN

(OR DON'T)

Ever watch someone catch a break, seemingly out of nowhere? They land a dream job they didn't even apply for, clinch a massive business deal that just "fell into their lap," or simply seem to have things effortlessly go their way, time and again. And what's the first thing you hear from the sidelines? "Man, they're so lucky." Or maybe you've thought it yourself, wishing you had a sprinkle of that magic fairy dust that seems to bless others. Let's be real, the idea of pure, unadulterated luck is incredibly comforting. It conveniently absolves you from the relentless grind, the hard choices, and the uncomfortable self-reflection. It allows you to believe that success is just a matter of chance, and if you haven't won yet, then you're just not one of the lucky ones. It keeps you a passive observer in your own life.

But here's the truth, and it's a hard one for some folks to swallow, because it puts the ball squarely back in their court:

What most people call luck is often an illusion. It's the shimmering mirage you see when someone's been relentlessly stacking the deck in their favor, consciously and unconsciously, piece by painstaking piece, over a long period. True luck, the kind that has absolutely nothing to do with your effort, mindset, grind, or personal development, is a purely random, unearned, and effortless positive outcome. It's the universe just deciding, for no discernible reason at all, to drop a gift in your lap.

Let me break bread and allow you to chew on this kind of pure, unadulterated, statistical anomaly "luck": Luck is when you bend down to tie your shoelace on a random Tuesday morning, only to find a legitimate, winning lottery ticket fluttering against your shoelaces, right there on the sidewalk. Not one you bought, not one you even knew was part of a drawing, just... there. And it happens to be for the mega jackpot. You didn't even realize it was drawing day, didn't play a number, didn't invest a cent. That's the kind of outrageous, unearned "luck" we're talking about – the kind that has absolutely nothing to do with your preparation, your persistence, your personal growth, or any choice you made. That's real luck. And how often does that happen? Rarely. It's the exception, not the rule.

Now, let's talk about being fortunate. This is where your power truly lies. Being fortunate describes a favorable circumstance or condition that you find yourself in, which, more often than not, is a direct, undeniable result of your actions, choices, preparation, and consistent effort. It's when you've intelligently and strategically positioned yourself for good outcomes, when the universe aligns not randomly, but in response to your relentless building, your unwavering commitment to growth. It's not passive; it's profoundly proactive, a direct consequence of your internal operating system.

And this is precisely where **Resilience, Growth Mindset, and Discipline (RGD)** become the undisputed architects of your fortunate life. As I always tell people, you don't luck your way through life, hoping for a random winning ticket. You actively, deliberately put yourself in a position to be fortunate. You create the conditions for good things to happen.

Think about it: when you've got **Resilience**, you don't just bounce back from every setback, every slammed door, every "no"; you spring forward, stronger and wiser, each time. You're still in the game, still standing, still fighting when the next opportunity finally flies by, ready and able to seize it.

Most people quit after the first few hits; the resilient ones remain when the real opportunities arise.

When you cultivate a **Growth Mindset**, you're constantly learning, adapting, seeing challenges not as dead ends but as puzzles to solve, new skills to acquire, and hidden lessons to uncover. This sharpens your vision, so you spot opportunities that the closed-minded, pessimistic individuals just walk right past, utterly oblivious to the potential right in front of them. And **Discipline**? That's the engine. That's the consistent, often unsexy, unglamorous work of building skills, mastering crafts, and relentlessly laying the foundation. Like the grinding hours I spent learning **CAD** in a damn prison. The endless appeals. The quiet, stubborn work of rebuilding my life after release, brick by brick. None of that felt "lucky." It felt like grueling work, like building my fortune one carefully placed brick at a time, sometimes with blood, sweat, and tears.

They say, "Luck is when preparation meets opportunity." What that means is you're building the damn preparation, day in and day out. You're honing your skills, sharpening your mind, expanding your knowledge, and refusing to quit, even when exhaustion screams for you to stop. So, when the "opportunity" finally shows its face – and they always do, if you're looking and ready – you're not fumbling around, unprepared, surprised. You're ready to seize it with both hands, to squeeze every drop of potential out of it, to maximize its value. To the outside observer, who hasn't seen the years of unseen effort, it looks like magic, like pure luck. But to the person who put in the deliberate, consistent work, it feels like an inevitability. It feels like earned fortune.

The Fortunate Few: Built, Not Born

Let's examine some everyday scenarios where RGD doesn't just meet opportunity; it actively cultivates it, or at the very least, ensures you're ready when opportunity knocks and positioned to make the most of it.

● **The "Unexpected Promotion" Story:** Meet Sarah. She's been in her role for years, not just doing the bare minimum, but quietly taking on extra projects, constantly seeking feedback (a prime example of Growth Mindset), and consistently delivering high-quality work, even when it's tedious and unappreciated (pure **Discipline**). One day, a senior position opens up suddenly due to an unforeseen departure. To everyone else, it appears to be a matter of "lucky timing" for Sarah.

But was it? No. Her **Discipline** had her consistently outperforming and preparing. Her growth mindset enabled her to learn adjacent skills, making her versatile and indispensable. Her **Resilience** meant she hadn't quit when things got tough earlier in her career, staying engaged and ready for the next level. She wasn't just lucky the role opened up; she was fortunate to have meticulously prepared herself for it, making herself the undeniable, obvious choice. The opportunity didn't randomly pick her; her **RGD** made her the perfect match for the chance.

● **The "Overnight Success" Myth:** You see an artist, an entrepreneur, or a content creator seemingly explode onto the scene. "They just got lucky with that one viral post/song/product," someone superficially says. What you didn't see were the thousands of hours they spent honing their craft (intense **Discipline**), experimenting with different styles and platforms (iterative **Growth Mindset)**, enduring countless rejections, criticism, and failures (unwavering **Resilience**), and creating a massive body of work, often for years, unseen.

That "viral post" wasn't luck; it was the fortuitous convergence of their relentless preparation meeting a fleeting, unpredictable moment in the algorithm or market.

They were fortunate to have built the necessary foundation, making them receptive to that "lucky" break and capable of capitalizing on it.

● **The "Always Finds a Solution" Friend:** We all know someone who seems to always land on their feet, no matter the crisis. Their car breaks down in the middle of nowhere, and within an hour, they've somehow rigged a temporary fix or found someone with a spare part and a tow. Is it luck that the right person drove by or that they remembered that obscure car trick? No, it's their **Resilience** kicking in, refusing to panic and embracing the challenge as a problem to be solved. It's their **Growth Mindset** that quickly analyzes the situation, drawing on past experiences and recalling obscure knowledge or creative solutions.

It's their **Discipline** of consistently maintaining their vehicle, or perhaps building a robust, mutually supportive network of contacts over time. They're not lucky to avoid disaster; they're fortunate to possess the mental fortitude and practical habits that enable them to navigate it effectively.

These aren't stories of random fortune falling from the sky like manna. These are stories of individuals who, often painfully and consciously, built their internal operating system using **RGD**. They weren't sitting around waiting for

149

a break; they were busy identifying, preparing for, and actively creating their opportunities for rest. A **Growth Mindset** helps you see the potential in a situation others dismiss as impossible. **Resilience** keeps you in the game long enough for those potentials to ripen and for true opportunities to emerge. And **Discipline** ensures you have the capacity, the skill, and the readiness to seize them.

Conversely, think about someone who lacks **RGD**. They might even stumble into a few "lucky" breaks, a random inheritance, or an easy job. However, without **Resilience** to overcome inevitable failures, a growth mindset to adapt and learn from setbacks, or **Discipline** to consistently capitalize on opportunities, those moments become wasted chances. They don't know how to capture the moment, extract its full potential, or transform potential into tangible results. They fumble the ball, time and again, letting opportunities slip through their fingers. It may appear to like chronic "bad luck" to them, reality just profound lack of the inner tools needed to turn potential into reality. They are not positioned to be fortunate.

The Unlucky Life Sentence, The Earned Freedom

Let's get one thing straight—luck didn't get me out of prison. I was staring down a life sentence with an imaginary release date of **"99/98/9999"**—a symbolic eternity. That's not a typo. It was a slap in the face. A reminder that I was never supposed to leave. Luck didn't get me out of that concrete cage. I had to learn the law, something utterly foreign to me, a street kid who'd never even seen a law book, let alone passed the bar. Even the expensive lawyers had nothing left—they'd already tried every conventional appeal—dead end. My appeals were stuck in the mud, seemingly destined to be buried forever, alongside my hopes.

There was no magic wand, no sudden intervention. It took **RGD**—raw **Resilience** to keep fighting after every denial, every slammed legal door, every crushing setback; a fierce **Growth Mindset** to believe I could learn complex legal jargon and navigate arcane procedures even without formal education; and the brutal **Discipline** to study every damn night, poring over dense legal texts others would find mind-numbingly dull and impossible. I fought my way out of that cage, relying on my faith and an unshakeable belief that I had truly changed, that I deserved a different future. I put myself in a position to be fortunate enough to walk free, because I earned it, inch by painful inch.

And the new skills? There was no luck involved in learning how to operate a **CNC** machine or mastering complex AutoCAD software and intricate G-codes in a prison vocational program. That was me, actively recognizing an opportunity within a grim situation, and putting in nearly fifteen years of complex, focused, consistent **Discipline** to master something utterly alien to my past. That wasn't luck; that was me actively building a new future for myself, ensuring I was fortunate enough to seize any chance that came my way upon release, not just idly hoping for one.

After nearly twenty-seven years, I walked out literally with nothing but the clothes on my back and a grim determination. No ID, no proof of who I was, no understanding of a world that had leapfrogged forward with cell phones and technology that didn't even exist when I went in. There was no luck in painstakingly relearning how to navigate society, how to apply for and land a good-paying job, how to rebuild my credit from scratch, or how to eventually buy my car and, yes, my own home.

That was the relentless, day-in, day-out application of **RGD**: changing my mindset, staying true to my principles and Integrity, and refusing to break even when the average person might have crumbled under the weight of such overwhelming obstacles and the temptation to revert to old ways. Yeah, I questioned myself. Doubts crept in. But I kept pushing, consciously building my fortunate life, one principled decision at a time.

Luck didn't make me a believer. Hard work, grit, and enduring through countless failures made me a believer. A profound and fundamental change in my mentality made me a believer. Luck only shows up when you've already built the foundation, when you've prepared yourself for the moment, when you're ready to receive it. The opportunities came, yes, they always do when you're positioned for them, but it was my transformation, my **RGD**, that allowed me to kick the door down and run right through it, propelled by faith and an unyielding belief in myself. It allowed me to be fortunate. So, stop waiting for luck. Start building your fortune.

The Unshakeable Foundation: A Blueprint Revisited

You've walked through fire with me through these pages so far. You've seen the relentless grip of adversity, the blinding allure of the streets, the silent torment of a ghost name and an impossible release date. You've witnessed the battles fought, both external and internal, the heavy cost of compromising my Integrity, and the deep peace that came with reclaiming it. But more importantly, you've seen the transformation that is possible. You've understood that the grit of my past wasn't just a story; it was a brutal yet essential education in building an unshakeable foundation for life—a blueprint for anyone seeking true freedom.

We've broken down **Resilience, Growth Mindset, and Discipline (RGD)** piece by piece. You've seen how **Resilience** isn't just bouncing back from a hit; it's about springing forward, stronger and wiser, from every single blow, transforming pain into power. You've learned how a **Growth Mindset** turns seemingly insurmountable obstacles into raw material for self-mastery, making you smarter from every stumble, a lifelong student of your potential. And you've seen how **Discipline**—the consistent, often thankless, unglamorous work of showing up and doing what needs to be done—is the quiet engine that turns raw potential into real results, pushing you past temporary pain to lasting power and profound peace.

We've stripped away the comforting illusion of "luck," showing how true success isn't about random chance, but about positioning yourself, preparing yourself, and then kicking the damn door down when opportunity finally shows its face. And we've hammered home the profound, liberating truth of Integrity, proving that the clearest conscience, living aligned with your values, is the ultimate freedom, a peace no external circumstance can ever buy or take away.

This isn't just my story of getting out of prison and rebuilding a life from zero. It's a universal blueprint for your life, no matter what cage you feel trapped in. Whether your walls are built of debt, bad habits, toxic relationships, crippling fear, or just that nagging, self-defeating voice in your head, the principles are the same, the path to liberation is internal. When you genuinely establish that **RGD**-fueled mentality, when you stop battling yourself and start aligning your thoughts, choices, and actions with your true potential, something incredible happens: you unlock a stress-free life. Yeah, I said it—less stress.

Because when your mind isn't a battlefield, when your conscience is clear, when you truly trust your ability to adapt, learn, and overcome any challenge, you think clearly. You make better decisions. You're not constantly looking over your shoulder or wrestling with internal demons of regret and self-doubt. That's not just good for your head; it's damn good for your body too. Less stress means less wear and tear, more energy, greater vitality, and a whole lot more peace that permeates every aspect of your existence. It's the ultimate upgrade for your mental and physical well-being.

Look, I didn't just survive. I learned to thrive. I went from staring at an imaginary release date to owning my own home, from battling my demons of self-sabotage to finding profound peace and purpose. And if an ex-con with no ID, no money, and no social connections can do it after **27 years** away from society, just imagine what you can achieve with the **RGD** principles under your belt. The path won't always be smooth, the challenges will still come, but the tools are here. The wisdom is here. The undeniable proof is here.

This book isn't just meant to entertain or to educate. It's intended to empower you. It's intended to light a fire under your ass and show you the immense, untapped power you already possess to change your life. And here's the real gem: Mastering **RGD** doesn't just change your life—it ripples outward. You become a beacon. You become the living proof for others that change is possible, that adversity can be conquered, and that true freedom is an inside job, built brick by disciplined brick. Your journey, fueled by **RGD**, becomes a ripple effect, inspiring those around you to discover their strength and forge their fortune.

As you continue this journey with me and consider what lies ahead, what's stopping you from taking the next step toward unleashing your own unbreakable life? Because if I can do it, you damn sure can.

One last thing—what's holding you back? The story you keep telling yourself. It's time to flip the script, time to write a new one—a tale of earned fortune, of unbreakable spirit, of ultimate freedom. And the next chapter awaits.

CHAPTER 7

THE DAILY UNLEASHING – LIVING YOUR RGD BLUEPRINT

Y ou've read my story. You've walked the path of adversity with me, navigated the chaos of the streets, and endured the cold steel of a prison cell. You've grappled with the illusion of "luck" and understood the profound, liberating freedom that comes with uncompromising Integrity. We've meticulously laid out the robust framework of **Resilience, Growth Mindset, and Discipline (RGD).**

Let's be clear from the jump: this book isn't here just to prop you up. It's not a quick pick-me-up or a one-time boost This **RGD** blueprint is here to do something far more profound and permanent: it's here to uplift you. It's designed to instill in you that unwavering confidence, that unshakeable inner strength, that sheer, indomitable will that gives you wings to fly and soar to the highest potential you can be. This is about igniting the raw power already inside you—to awaken the better version of yourself, the one you've barely scratched the surface off. It's here to crack open this beautiful, messy life, open your mind, give you a broader perspective, deeper understanding, and the knowledge and fierce will to be that great person you were always meant to be.

This isn't a book to sit on your shelf, gathering dust bunnies and silent judgments. No, my friend. This is a living, breathing blueprint for the rest of your damn life, a battle plan for continuous self-mastery. And the real work – the thrilling, transformative work – begins the moment you turn this final page, with the daily unleashing of your unbreakable self.

Remember that unshakeable foundation we talked about in the last chapter, the very core you're building? **RGD** isn't something you forge once and then forget about, like a forgotten gym membership or a New Year's resolution that fades by February. It's a living, breathing, evolving operating system for your entire existence. The world, bless its chaotic heart, won't stop throwing curveballs. New "cages" will inevitably appear—a job loss that blindsides you, a personal setback that feels like a gut punch, an unexpected challenge that tests every fiber of your resolve. The fundamental difference now is that you've the tools. You know how to face them down, not just survive, but truly thrive, to use every obstacle as fuel for your growth.

Your Daily RGD Workout: Forging the Unbreakable You

So, what does it truly mean to live this blueprint, day in and day out? It's about consistently applying those three mighty pillars in the small, often unseen moments, because it's precisely in these small moments that true, profound transformation happens. They are the quiet, consistent drills that build your fortress from the inside out, layer by layer.

1. Resilience: The Daily Springboard

Resilience isn't just for the big falls; it's for the daily stumbles, the micro-frustrations, the unexpected annoyances that chip away at your peace. That infuriating email that makes your blood pressure spike? The unexpected bill that lands like a lead weight? The moment some random fool cuts you off in traffic and flips you off? These aren't just annoyances; they are all prime opportunities to practice your Resilience.

Instead of "crashing out"—reverting to old, destructive patterns of rage, blame, or defeat—take a deliberate, conscious breath. This pause is your power. Reframe the

160

irritation. Ask yourself: "What's the one tiny, almost laughable step I can take here to regain control?" or "What's the unexpected lesson in this annoyance, beyond just 'these sucks'?" It's in those micro-moments of choosing calm over chaos, of selecting a measured, principled response over an impulsive eruption, that your inner strength truly gets a consistent workout. You don't need a prison sentence or major disaster to build **Resilience**. Sometimes, a regular Tuesday—and the **Discipline** to choose differently—is enough.

• Micro-Action: The Three-Breath Pause. When something minor frustrates you today, before you even think of reacting or speaking, pause for three slow, deliberate breaths. This creates a tiny, powerful space for conscious choice, allowing your Resilience to kick in.

• Micro-Action: The Daily Lesson Log. At the end of your day, identify just one minor setback or irritation you faced. Actively list one thing you learned from it, or one tiny way you can approach it differently tomorrow. Journal it, even if it's just a sentence. This cultivates a **Growth Mindset** alongside **Resilience**.

2. Growth Mindset: The Daily Reframe

A Growth Mindset isn't just for learning new skills; it's for actively confronting and dismantling old, limiting beliefs that hold you captive. That sneaky voice that whispers "you're a loser, you'll never get out of this financial mess, you're stuck," or "you always mess this up, why even try?" That's your old, outdated programming trying to keep you small and "safe," sabotaging your potential.

Challenge it. Aggressively. Ask, "What if I can learn from this? What if this supposed 'failure' is a powerful teacher dressed in uncomfortable clothes, offering a hard-earned lesson?" Seek voices that rattle your comfort zone and shake up your usual way of thinking. Read something new and uncomfortable, listen to someone who feels completely different, someone who makes your brain itch in a good way. Every conversation, every minor mistake, every piece of critical feedback becomes a vibrant opportunity to expand your mind, to debug that old, flawed moral code we discussed. This is the constant sharpening of your mental edge, making you adaptable, innovative, and truly formidable.

● Micro-Action: The Uncomfortable Curiosity. For one hour today, intentionally listen to a podcast or read an article on a topic entirely new for you, one that makes you slightly uncomfortable or challenges a deeply held belief. To expand your frame of reference and cultivate genuine curiosity.

● Micro-Action: The "What If This Works?" Inquiry. When you feel yourself resisting a new idea, a significant change, or a perceived challenge, catch yourself. Then, actively ask: "What if this works? What are the positive possibilities if I lean into this?" and genuinely explore those possibilities, even for a few minutes. This primes your mind for growth.

3. Discipline: The Daily Accumulator

Discipline isn't loud. It's that quiet voice choosing the hard thing when no one's watching. It's those tiny, gritty choices that stack up into unshakable strength. It's that unsexy, everyday grind that nobody applauds, but that quietly builds empires and fortifies your inner world. It's waking up 15 minutes earlier to plan your day, instead of hitting snooze and scrambling. It's choosing the nutritious, energy-giving meal when the junk food is screaming your name and offering instant, fleeting gratification. It's following through on a promise you made to yourself, even when no one else is watching, especially when no one else is watching.

Every single time you choose the hard right over the easy wrong, every time you delay gratification for a greater, long-term reward, you're actively forging a stronger, more reliable, more trustworthy version of yourself. Each small win sharpens your edge. Stack them, and you build a momentum that doesn't quit—and a self-trust that can't be broken. They are the quiet acts that scream, louder than any megaphone: "I am in control of my destiny."

● Micro-Action: The Smallest Uncomfortable Task First. Pick one small, uncomfortable task you've been avoiding today (e.g., making that difficult call, tidying that messy drawer, replying to that one email, starting that challenging workout) and commit to completing it first, before anything else. Get it done.

● Micro-Action: The 5-Minute Commitment. Commit to one specific, healthy habit for just 5 minutes today (e.g., stretching, meditating, tidying your space, reading a motivational passage). The consistency of the action, not the duration, is the undeniable key to building lasting **Discipline**

Building Your RGD Ecosystem: Your Circle of Strength

You don't have to walk this path alone, even if the core change is an inside job. Your environment and the people you surround yourself with are powerful forces, for good or for ill. Just as I consciously stepped away from toxic influences in prison to protect my newfound mindset, you need to cultivate your own "**RGD** Ecosystem" on the outside. This is your personal support network, your mental nutrition, your fortress defense.

Seek out:

• Mentors: Not just people who inspire you from afar, but those who have genuinely achieved what you aspire to, and who embody **RGD** principles in their own lives. Their wisdom, shortcuts, battle-tested advice, and ability to identify your blind spots can save you years of trial and error and a great deal of unnecessary pain.

• Accountability Partners: A trusted friend, a family member, a coach, or a group who genuinely understands your goals and can help you stay honest and consistent. Someone who will call you on your B.S. with tough love, not judgment, and celebrate your progress with genuine enthusiasm.

• Positive Influences: Ruthlessly prune your social circles, if necessary. Surround yourself with individuals who uplift you, challenge you constructively, and genuinely believe in growth, possibility, and solution-finding, rather than dwelling on misery, gossip, or stagnant comfort zones. These are the people who will celebrate your tiny victories and help you learn from your inevitable stumbles without judgment.

• Nourishing Content: Be a ruthless gatekeeper of your mind. Feed it with books, podcasts, documentaries, and courses that inspire, educate, and actively reinforce your **RGD** mindset. Just as much as you control your thoughts, you control what information and energy you allow into your mental space. Whatever you feed your mind grows. Starve the nonsense. Fuel the truth. Choose your inputs wisely.

Avoiding negative people, energy-draining situations, or toxic content isn't weakness; it's simply smart, strategic Discipline. It's protecting your hard-won mental peace, because a strong mentality is like a fortress; you don't invite saboteurs through the gates. This ain't about being judgmental or holier-than-thou; it's about being discerning and protecting your invaluable investment in yourself and your future.

The Continuous Pursuit of Freedom: Your Life, Unleashed

My freedom didn't stop the day I walked out of those prison gates. It was just the opening act of a whole new kind of hustle: the relentless, daily pursuit of an uncaged mind, a life of continuous growth and contribution. And that's exactly what's waiting for you, right now. You have the inherent power to break free from self-doubt, from crippling past regrets, from the limiting stories you've inherited or unknowingly created.

This book is a guide, a map, a collection of battle-tested truths, but your life is the laboratory. Go out there. Experiment. Fail. Fall. Get back up. Learn. Grow. Celebrate every small win, every tiny step forward—they are the irrefutable proof of your progress. Don't let setbacks derail you; see them as feedback, as detours that teach you more about the terrain than the straight road ever could.

Understand that the accurate measure of your strength isn't that you never break. It's that every single time you're tested, every single time you face a challenge, you come back unshakeable, better, stronger, and more truly free.

The journey won't always be easy. Let's be real; there will be days when the old temptations whisper sweet nothings in your ear, when the daily grind feels overwhelmingly pointless, when you question everything and everyone, including yourself. But in those moments, remember where you've been, and remember the powerful tools you now possess. Remember that man who faced an imaginary release date and built his way out, brick by painstaking brick. If he could do it, you can damn sure conquer your challenges.

Your unleashed life isn't some distant dream. It's a choice you make—right now, and every damn day after. So, get it.

A FINAL THOUGHT AS YOU BEGIN YOUR UNLEASHING...

This book, this particular blueprint, concludes here. But know that the conversation on mastering your potential, on forging an even stronger you, is far from over. There are always new depths to explore, new challenges to conquer, and new ways to unleash the immense power within you.

Keep an eye out, because the journey to true self-mastery is an ongoing one, and I've got more to share on that path.

www.ingramcontent.com/pod-product-compliance
Lightning Source LLC
Chambersburg PA
CBHW071748120626
46550CB00002B/709